Philosophy: Key Themes

Philosophy: Key Themes

Julian Baggini

First published 2002 by
PALGRAVE MACMILLAN
Houndmills, Basingstoke, Hampshire RG21 6XS and
175 Fifth Avenue, New York, N.Y. 10010
Companies and representatives throughout the world

PALGRAVE MACMILLAN is the global academic imprint of the Palgrave
Macmillan division of St. Martin's Press, LLC and of Palgrave Macmillan Ltd.
Macmillan® is a registered trademark in the United States, United Kingdom
and other countries. Palgrave is a registered trademark in the European
Union and other countries.

ISBN 0–333–96486–1 hardcover
ISBN 0–333–96487–X paperback

This book is printed on paper suitable for recycling and made from fully
managed and sustained forest sources.

A catalogue record for this book is available from the British Library.

Library of Congress Cataloging-in-Publication Data

Baggini, Julian.
    Philosophy : key themes / Julian Baggini.
        p. cm.
    Includes bibliographical references (p.) and index.
    ISBN 0–333–96486–1 — ISBN 0–333–96487–X (pbk.)
    1. Philosophy.   I. Title.

B72 .B333 2002
100—dc21

                                                           2002074840

10   9   8   7   6   5   4
11   10   09   08   07   06   05   04

Printed in China

For Claudia and Richard

Contents

3   Philosophy of Mind   61

4   Philosophy of Religion   86

Preface

This book is designed to help the reader approach five key themes in Western philosophy. Its aim is to give brief, accurate and informative overviews of the major arguments given and positions held in each area.

The introduction contains some advice on how to read and make sense of philosophical arguments. Philosophy is not a museum of ideas or an intellectual pick and mix. Arguments need to be carefully examined and assessed and this section helps provide some of the tools to do this.

Each chapter comprises a discussion of the main areas in each theme, a summary, a glossary of key terms and suggestions for further reading.

The discussions combine two main features. First, they summarise and explain the main arguments of each theme, clarifying and distilling their core. Second, the discussions also contain critical points, questioning the validity or soundness of arguments, and highlighting potential weaknesses and problems in the positions examined. The main purpose of this is not to provide an exhaustive catalogue of criticisms, but to highlight potential weaknesses and to encourage the reader to question the claims being made for themselves.

There is also a glossary of key philosophical words at the end of the book, along with suggestions for further reading in philosophy.

Acknowledgements

Thanks to Terka Acton, Penny Simmons and the anonymous readers at the publishers who helped make this book possible and then better than it otherwise would have been. Thanks also are due to my students whose feedback on the teaching materials that formed the bases of this book encouraged me to develop them further.

Acknowledgements

Introduction

If you went to a driving school, you might well expect to be taught about the highway code and some basics about car maintenance, but what you'd expect to spend most of your time doing would be actually learning to drive. If you pick up an introduction to philosophy or enrol on a philosophy course, however, you'll find that you spend a lot of time being presented with philosophical arguments but very little time, if any at all, learning how to actually philosophise. The presumption seems to be that to do philosophy, you just have to dive into some of it and find your way around yourself.

Being thrown in at the deep end is not always the best way to learn and even being thrown in at the shallow end, which is what happens to most readers of introductions, is not much better. So before going on to discuss the five themes covered in this book, this introduction will give you a crash course in the basic skills of philosophising. Of course, these skills will be best developed when applied to the arguments presented in the rest of the book. But at the very least, they should give you a head start in being able to make the most of them.

▶ Where do we start?

One of philosophy's distinguishing features is that it questions everything and assumes nothing. Philosophy exposes and questions the assumptions which underlie our everyday thinking about the world, ourselves, our values and our beliefs.

But at the same time, one cannot always be questioning everything or else we would only ever be able to consider the most fundamental questions in philosophy. These questions include many of those discussed in the chapter on theory of knowledge, such as how we can have knowledge and whether the external world exists or not. These are vital questions in philosophy. But if we are considering, for example, the question of the mind's relation to the body, we will get nowhere fast if we insist we first have to justify our belief in the existence of an external reality.

So although it is true that philosophy questions everything and assumes nothing, this questioning has to be kept in its place. The time to question the existence of the external world is when we are doing epistemology (theory of knowledge) or metaphysics, not usually when we are doing the philosophy of mind.

The problem is that there is no formula for determining which questions should be put to one side and which are central to the issue being discussed. Here, as with so much in philosophy, good judgement is required. Unfortunately, good judgement is more like a knack one needs to develop than a technique that can be directly taught.

Nevertheless, merely being aware of the problem is a good start. Too often people start doing philosophy and come to think that a few easy points can be scored by simply questioning any assumption an argument rests upon. But except when we are considering the most basic questions of philosophy (and perhaps even then too), we always need to make some assumptions to even get started. The question is whether these are appropriate or inappropriate assumptions to make.

▶ Premises

Some people say that philosophy is about ideas. In fact, it's more accurate to say that philosophy is about arguments. It's no good having what sounds like a great philosophical idea – for example, that we have no free will, or that everything in the universe is composed of one single substance – unless you can provide arguments to support it. Arguments are basically rational justifications for conclusions. There are many ways in which this process of rational justification can proceed. But before we even get to that stage, we have to start with what the argument is arguing from – premises.

The premises of an argument are those fundamentals which have to be accepted as true in order for the justification to get started. For example, consider the argument that God cannot exist because there is evil in the world and a good, all-powerful God would not let this happen (see Chapter 4). There are at least three premises required for this argument: that if God exists, God is all-powerful; that if God exists, God is Good and loving; and that there is evil in the world. From these three premises, the argument tries to demonstrate that God cannot exist. In other words, the premises are used to provide a rational justification for the conclusion that God doesn't exist. But if one rejects any of these premises, the argument cannot work. If you think there is no evil in the world, for example, the argument fails to get off the ground.

How does one decide whether to accept the premises of an argument? There is no simple answer to this. Sometimes, we are asked to accept a premise on the basis of evidence. In this example, it just does seem to be true that there is evil – in some sense of the word – in the world. To say that there isn't flies in the face of the evidence of the holocaust, genocides and other terrible acts recorded in history. On other occasions, we are asked to accept premises on conceptual grounds. In the example above, it just does seem to be an essential part of the concept of God that God is all-powerful and all-loving. Some premises are justified on the grounds of basic logic. The fact that something cannot both be and not be at the same time, for example, is an elementary logical truth. And sometimes we are asked to accept a premise because it is itself the conclusion of another argument.

Sometimes premises are stated clearly, on other occasions they are tacitly assumed. In either case, when assessing an argument one needs to be able to identify what its premises are and whether they should be accepted. Only then should you move on to consider whether the rational justification is sufficient for the conclusion.

▶ Forms of rational justification

All arguments move from premises to conclusions, but there are different ways of making this movement. The three most important forms are deduction, induction and abduction.

Deduction is the most rigorous of the three. In a deductive argument, the movement from premises to conclusion should be as precise and as rigorous as in a mathematical sum. Just as $1 + 1 = 2$, no dispute, so in a deductive argument premise + premise = conclusion, no dispute. Consider as an example:

Brechin City is the greatest football team in Britain.
Roddy Grant plays for Brechin City.
Therefore, Roddy Grant plays for the greatest football team in Britain.

Note that in an argument such as this, 'therefore' stands in the same relation to the premises and conclusion that ' = ' does to the sum and its product.

In this example, it should be clear that the conclusion follows from the premises as surely as 2 is the sum of $1 + 1$. This means that if the premises are true, the conclusion must also be true. Such an argument is said to be valid. That does not mean, however, that the conclusion has been shown to be true. Its truth is only demonstrated if the premises are true. (In this example, it seems sadly to be the case that at least one of the premises is not true.) If the premises are true and the argument is valid, then the argument is sound. A sound argument is a philosophical bull's-eye.

Because deductive arguments are the most rigorous of all arguments, it is ideal if one can justify one's conclusions by using them. However, it is not always possible to employ a deductive argument, for reasons that will become clear when we look at the second form of argument: induction.

Inductive arguments do not have the same necessary link between the truths of the premises and the conclusions. In an inductive argument, the premises are considered to be good evidence for the truth of the conclusion but not a guarantee of its truth. Take the following as an example:

No-one has ever run 100 metres in less than 9.7 seconds.
Jenny Jones is running 100 metres tomorrow.
Therefore, Jenny Jones will not run 100 metres in less than 9.7 seconds tomorrow.

The conclusion of this argument may seem so secure that you'd bet your last dollar on it. But the conclusion does not follow with any necessity from the premises. It is possible that both the premises are true and yet the conclusion is false – Jenny Jones could confound us all and run an amazing 100 metres. The argument is thus deductively invalid.

However, on this occasion, the fact that the argument is invalid probably doesn't bother us. We don't require the conclusion to follow as a matter of necessity from the premises. It is enough that the premises give us overwhelmingly good reasons to accept the conclusion. Inductive arguments, therefore, do not require the same rigorous standard of proof as deductive ones.

Why should we ever accept one of these inductive arguments if they are less rigorous than deductive ones? The answer is that we often have no choice. When we reason about matters of fact, we have to base our arguments on experience of the past. This experience is always limited, in that we cannot know everything that has happened in the past and we do not have experience of what will happen in the future. None the less, we assume that the unobserved past, present and future will resemble the observed past and present in certain vital respects. Unless we did this, we would be unable to make any generalisations about the world about us. But any generalisation about the world based on our limited experience has to fail the test of deductive validity. That is because all such arguments are basically of the form:

Every time we have observed X in the past, Y has been true of X.
Therefore, Y is true of X in the future and the unobserved past.

Clearly, this is an invalid argument. But if we didn't reason in this way, we would not be able to conclude that, for instance, all water freezes at zero degrees centigrade, or all people are mortal. In both these cases, as in all other generalisations about matters of fact, we are making a generalisation about all cases on the basis of a limited, though often large, number of other cases.

There are many interesting and important philosophical disputes about the status and justification of inductive arguments. All we need to be clear about here is that they do have their place and that they differ in their justification from deductive ones. They are not valid, but we still have to judge whether the premises provide sufficient evidence to justify the conclusions.

A third form of argument is known as abduction. This is often known by its more descriptive name 'argument to the best explanation'. For example, several years back people discovered strange markings in fields. These so-called 'crop circles' seemed to appear overnight, from nowhere. Where did they come from?

No deductive argument could help here. From the fact that these circles existed and no-one knew where they came from, no facts about their origins could be deduced by means of a valid argument. Standard inductive arguments were also inadequate, since no past experiences directly corresponded to these new phenomena. The only alternative way to reason was by abduction, where we look for the best explanation of the phenomenon.

In this case, the main candidates were alien visitations, human pranksters, or natural forces such as wind vortexes. The evidence would later show which of these explanations fitted the facts, so eventually induction provided the solution. But before this evidence settled the matter, we could only ask which hypothesis best explained their appearance.

Here, abduction provided a temporary, provisional solution until enough evidence could be gathered for an inductive explanation. But when it comes to issues such as whether God exists, or whether other people have minds, we may have to rely permanently on arguments to the best explanation. This form of argument is the best kind of rational account we can give for a conclusion if it cannot be demonstrated by a deductive argument or if there is insufficient evidence to construct an inductive one.

Deduction, induction and abduction thus provide three models for arguments. Each provides a different way of producing a rational account which justifies the drawing of a conclusion from premises. One needs to be able to recognise when each type of argument is being used, whether it is appropriate that it is being used in the context, and whether it is satisfactorily executed.

▶ Critiquing arguments

What has been sketched out so far provides only a brief account of the basics of philosophical argumentation. However, if one takes on board all the lessons from it, one is provided with a wide range of tools for the critique of arguments.

First, one can show that the argument depends upon a false premise. This attacks the argument at its root and prevents it from getting off the ground. Sometimes, it is necessary to show that a premise is actually false. On other occasions, it can be enough to show that the premise has not been established. For instance, if one wants to argue that baboons should be granted full human rights because they demonstrate the capacity for abstract thought, the argument fails if the truth of the premise has not been established. One doesn't need to show that baboons don't have the capacity for abstract thought, it is enough to show that it has not been established that they do. (The argument that we should grant baboons full human rights because they *might* have the capacity for abstract thought is importantly different.)

Second, one can show that the argument depends upon a premise which has not been recognised and is either false or not established as true. For example, in the baboon argument, it may simply have been assumed by the person putting forward the argument that full human rights should be granted to creatures that can demonstrate the capacity for abstract thought. If this is so, then the argument rests on an unstated and unrecognised premise. The critic can then show that this premise is in fact necessary for the argument to work and then show that it is either false or has not been shown to be true.

Third, if the argument is deductive in structure, one can show that the argument is invalid. One does this by showing that the premises do not guarantee the truth of the conclusion. For example, someone might argue:

If John got drunk last night, he'll look a wreck this morning.
John looks a wreck this morning.
Therefore, John got drunk last night.

This can be shown to be invalid because it is possible that both premises are true yet the conclusion is false. For instance, it may be true that John always looks a wreck in the morning if he gets drunk the night before and that John looks a wreck this morning, but in this instance he looks terrible because his neighbours kept him awake all night playing Johnny Mathis albums at full volume, not because he got drunk. Therefore the argument is invalid. (Note that the argument is invalid even if, as a matter of fact, Johnny did get drunk last night. The point is the conclusion doesn't follow from the premises and so is not necessarily true, not that it is necessarily false.)

Fourth, in an inductive argument one can show that the premises do not provide sufficient evidence for the conclusion. If I reason that everyone who has ever lived has died and therefore I too will die, this is a justifiable inference. But if I reason that everyone I've ever met called Simon has been an arrogant fool and that therefore everyone called Simon is an arrogant fool, this is clearly not a justifiable inference. What makes an inductive inference justifiable is a matter of debate, but it essentially hinges upon the argument being based on the kind of evidence which can reliably be generalised from. A limited acquaintance with a few people with the same name is not the kind of evidence from which one can generalise to all people with the same name.

Fifth, in an abductive argument one can argue that there is a better explanation than the one offered. One can do this by showing that the alternative explains more, relies on fewer coincidences or makes fewer assumptions, for example. In the crop circles example, the explanation that winds caused the circles requires one to suppose that freak weather caused some remarkably intricate patterns to be created. That seems as likely as imagining that a great abstract painting was caused by the chance spillages of some paint buckets. The explanation that hoaxers did it explains more because it explains not only the appearance of the circles, but also their intricate design.

Sixth, one can argue that an inappropriate or inadequate form of justification has been used. Different issues call for different types of argument. In some cases the firm proof of a deductive argument may be needed, but only an inductive argument is offered. This is most evident when someone is offering an argument as a firm proof but the argument fails to be deductively valid. One might also criticise someone for trying to provide a deductive argument when the subject matter demands an inductive one. Matching the right form of argument to the right issue is a skill as important as constructing one's arguments well.

▶ Beyond demolition

From what has been said so far, it may seem that examining philosophical arguments is a rather negative enterprise. The focus has been on critique and finding mistakes. But surely the aim is to hit upon the truth, not simply to pull apart arguments?

It is certainly true that philosophy is not just a negative enterprise. But it is wrong to see its critical aspects as being wholly negative. When we examine arguments from all sides and attempt to find faults in them, we do not (or at least should not) do so for the mere pleasure of finding fault. The function of such critical examination is more like the function of a quality control department in a factory. A company which spends a lot of its resources rigorously testing its own products to ensure they stand up to hard use is a company which is likely to produce superior goods. Philosophy Inc. hopefully follows this model. We examine arguments as rigorously as possible because we want the ones that do get out and enjoy an intellectual life to be as durable and effective as possible.

Nevertheless, more often than not it is decided that an argument doesn't quite make the grade. Does that mean it should simply be thrown out? Not at all. We can almost always learn from a close examination of an argument, even if we end up rejecting it. There are at least three ways of doing this.

First, the major arguments in philosophy have all, for some time at least, been put forward and believed by some of the smartest people in society. It is extremely unlikely that these people were wholly wrong. Even when an argument fails, there is usually at least a part of it which hits upon a truth. So it is always worth looking for the truth or insight which lies behind the flawed argument. For example, the behaviourist thesis that all mental concepts refer to behaviours rather than inner mental events does not have many supporters today. But a sympathetic reader will see that what motivated this view was the realisation that we need something public to fix the meaning of mental concepts for them to have any shared meaning at all (see Chapter 3). Seeing what is true in behaviourism is therefore essential if we are learn anything from it.

Second, if an argument is flawed, it may just be that it needs a little improving. For example, if one is arguing in applied ethics and one uses the premise 'It is always wrong to kill a human being' in an argument about euthanasia, most people would reject the argument, since very few people think it is always wrong to kill a human being. Self-defence, for example, may be an instance where killing is permitted. But instead of simply rejecting the argument, it can be much more fruitful to revise it. In this case, the premise could perhaps be revised to, 'It is always wrong to kill an innocent human being'. This process of revision and strengthening of the argument could go on for a long time. But unless one at least tries to construct the strongest possible argument for a position before rejecting it, one hasn't given that position a fair chance.

This point is particularly important in the context of a book like this, where each theme is only introduced. You will not read here the most sophisticated and elaborate arguments for the positions discussed simply because to have presented these would have changed the book from a brief introduction to a detailed, advanced text. Therefore, if one finds some of the arguments too simplistic and obviously wrong, that may well be as much a product of the relatively unsophisticated nature of the text as a lack of better arguments for the positions themselves.

A third reason to look beyond the failures of an argument is that, even if the argument is indeed irredeemable, we can often learn from its mistakes. The argument from design, for example, which attempts to show that God must exist because the universe is so orderly, is, most would agree, a poor argument (see Chapter 4). But understanding why it is poor increases one's understanding of how inductive arguments work and of the limits on arguments from analogy. We can learn from its inadequacies and should take the opportunity to do so.

▶ Becoming a philosopher

From what has been said so far, it should be clear that there is no difference between reading philosophy properly and doing philosophy. Hence, the skills a reader needs to develop are the skills of philosophising. To conclude, I will sum up what some of those skills are.

To be a philosopher one needs to treat the philosophy one reads, not as authoritative texts to be ingested and learned, but as one side of a conversation to be participated in. One needs to approach the text critically but constructively. A balance needs to be struck between looking for what might be wrong in the argument and looking for any truths or insights is may none the less contain.

It is important to go beyond exactly what is written on the page before you. One should try and see what is motivating the arguments, what unstated premises, if any, lie behind them, and how one might take the argument forward. What one reads is almost always a start for an enquiry and not the end.

If all this makes reading philosophy sound quite demanding, then that is only because, done properly, reading philosophy is demanding. Philosophy requires you to draw on all your intellectual resources for the intellect is the only resource we have to do philosophy with. However, though demanding, many find it rewarding, sometimes exhilarating even.

This book should provide a set of keys to unlock the door to some of philosophy's riches. As such it is an entrance only, but one that I hope you find yourself glad to have gone through.

1 Theory of Knowledge

▶ What is the theory of knowledge?

If I were to ask you whether you know anything, you might understandably find my question odd. Of course we know things. We know where we live and what our names are. We know that 2 + 2 = 4 and that the square root of 9 is 3. We know Rome is the capital of Italy, that there is a blackcurrant bush in the garden and that we had a cup of coffee for breakfast this morning. It's one of the basic facts about humans that they know things.

Philosophers have always found this common-sense idea rather problematic. Socrates is reputed to have gone so far as to say that the only thing he knew was that he knew nothing. How can we explain this stark contrast between common sense and the doubts of philosophers?

The root of the problem is that knowledge seems to require a special kind of certainty which ordinary belief doesn't have. But once you ask what could justify this certainty, you begin to find that it's very difficult, if not impossible, to find an answer.

It's easy to see why so many thinkers have argued that knowledge requires certainty. 'Know' is what we could call a success verb. 'Learn' is such a verb. To say someone has learned something is to say that they have studied it success-fully and have now taken on board whatever it is they were learning. (To say someone *is learning* obviously doesn't imply this mastery has been attained, only that it is being worked towards.) Another example of a success verb is 'remember'. To say someone has remembered something is to say that they have successfully recalled information about or acquired in the past.

Because such verbs imply success, it doesn't make sense to use them if success has not been achieved. To say someone has learned to speak Italian implies they can speak Italian, or at least could speak it before they got out of practice. If we 'remember' drinking coffee but in fact drank tea, then strictly speaking we didn't remember at all, but just seemed to remember. You can only genuinely remember what actually happened.

The success required to genuinely 'know' is disputed, but at minimum it implies that what we know is in fact true. I can't know that Auckland is the capital of New Zealand if the capital is in fact Wellington. I can only know that there is a blackcurrant bush in my garden if there is actually such a bush there.

When we are wrong about what we claim to know, we say that we merely believe, incorrectly. Beliefs can be true or false. But I can only *know* what is true.

This is where the problem comes in. If I am to claim to know anything, I should really only make such a claim when what I know is definitely true. If I can't be sure it is true, I should really say I believe it, not that I know it. This means that knowledge seems to require a certainty that what is known is actually true.

The problem, as we shall see throughout this chapter, is that such certainty is hard to come by. But if we can't find it, surely we can't claim to have knowledge?

The relationship between knowledge and belief will also be considered in more detail. We have seen that knowledge is not the same thing as belief, but there does seem to be a strong connection between the two. Knowledge seems to be a special kind of belief, belief which carries a seal of certainty.

The theory of knowledge (epistemology) is a central theme in philosophy. In some senses, all philosophy leads back to the question, what can we know? Hence, the considerations of this chapter are of interest to all themes in philosophy, not just epistemology.

To begin, we will consider a fundamental question in epistemology: where does our knowledge come from?

▶ Rationalism

A recurring theme in philosophy is the relationship between our minds and the world. Philosophers as different in their outlook as Descartes and Locke have agreed that it is our nature as thinking beings which distinguishes persons from animals and that philosophy is largely about the questions that arise in the minds of such beings when they consider how the faculty of thought works.

In epistemology, two different accounts of this faculty are offered by two traditions: rationalism and empiricism.

Rationalism is mostly closely associated with seventeenth- and eighteenth-century philosophers such as Descartes, Leibniz and Spinoza. However, the defining characteristics of rationalism can be detected in many thinkers before and after.

Rationalists believe that the way to attain knowledge is to rely on the resources of logic and the intellect. Such reasoning does not depend upon the data of experience, but proceeds from basic truths which do not require to be and are not grounded in experience. Such reasoning and the principles it starts with are described as *a priori*, since such reasoning is prior to experience. One example of an *a priori* proposition is that $1 + 1 = 2$. We can know this to be true just by thinking about what the sum means. We do not need to look and see if the real world provides evidence for or justifies the sum. Similarly, basic principles of logic such as 'nothing can both be and not be at the same time' are *a priori*, since they are not justified by, or grounded in, facts about the world.

The caricature of the rationalist as an 'armchair philosopher' is not wholly unjustified, since their approach to philosophy does suggest that all the important truths about reality can be discovered by thought alone, without any need to go off and examine the world.

Rationalism can appear a bit dotty to the modern mind, which is used to the idea that science, with its emphasis on experimentation and observation, is vital to the advance of knowledge. However, it can appear a little less cranky if one disabuses oneself of some common misconceptions about rationalism.

First, the rationalist does not say that one could reason without having had any experience whatsoever. We need to be taught language and educated properly if we are to have any chance of success in philosophy. The point is not that philosophers need have no experience at all of the outside world. It is rather that, once they have been equipped with good reasoning skills, language and a basic understanding of things like maths and geometry, they can go on to reason without any further reference to experience. Such *a priori* reasoning starts from first principles rather than from the evidence of experience.

Second, the rationalist does not say that one can discover particular facts about the world without going out into it. No-one could know how far London is from Paris, for example, without referring to the evidence of experience. But when it comes to knowledge about the most basic features of reality, such appeals to experience are not required. To know what the time is now, for example, I need a clock. But to understand the nature of time itself, I need only think carefully about the concept of time. To know what substance my kettle is made of, I need to test the metal it is made of. But to understand what the general nature of substance is, and whether mind and matter are different substances, I need only think carefully about what substance, mind and matter are.

To see how rationalism can be intuitively appealing, consider an example of a rationalist argument derived from an Ancient Greek philosopher, Zeno (*c*.470 BCE). There is a race between Achilles and a tortoise. Achilles runs quickly, the tortoise slowly, but constantly – he is never at rest. The tortoise has a head start. In order for Achilles to overtake the tortoise, he must first get to where the tortoise started from. This will take him a certain amount of time, during which the tortoise will have moved on, however slowly. At this point in time, then, the tortoise is still ahead of Achilles. For Achilles now to overtake the tortoise, he must once again first get to where the tortoise has moved on to. This takes him a period of time, however short, during which time the tortoise will have moved on a little more. Having got to where the tortoise was, to overtake, Achilles must once again first get to where the tortoise has moved on to, and so on. The point of the argument is to show that, according to what seems to be impeccable logic, Achilles can never overtake the tortoise.

At this point you might think that this is a terrible advertisement for armchair-style rationalism because we all know from experience that Achilles would have overtaken the tortoise. But the argument is not completed. It is true that Achilles would win the race. So what is wrong with the argument? One suggestion is that the argument depends on the assumption that you can divide up time and space into infinitely small parts. No matter how short a space of time you have or how short a distance, you can always talk about Achilles needing to travel that distance in a certain time. The argument thus depends upon the idea that space and time can be divided up into ever smaller parts.

So, in fact, the conclusion of the argument is not the absurdity that Achilles cannot overtake the tortoise, but the startling revelation that time and space cannot be infinitely divisible. So, it seems we have learned something about the fundamental nature of reality just by thinking in our armchairs.

This example is intended to show how rationalism may not seem quite so daft after all. However, it should be pointed out that the argument does require a small appeal to experience (the knowledge that people can overtake in races) and that Zeno also put forward arguments that showed time and space cannot consist of indivisible parts, directly contradicting the conclusion of this argument!

There are some other key features of rationalism which need to be highlighted. The first is that it takes as its model of rationality deductive reasoning (see Introduction). That is to say, one advances arguments by very precise steps, only accepting conclusions which strictly follow from the premises. The model here is mathematics, whereby every stage of the calculation has to be proved and where there is no room for guesswork or 'more or less' answers.

The second is that rationalism rests on the assumption that only one conception of reality will be consistent with the findings of reason. Just as only one answer is correct to any given sum in arithmetic, so the rationalist believes, if you reason properly, only one account of reality will fit the deductions of reason. If this weren't the case, then you could never be sure that you had arrived at a proper understanding of reality, since it would be possible that equally sound reasoning could have led you to a different conclusion.

This last assumption of rationalism has come under considerable attack. Most philosophers now believe that there are many accounts of ultimate reality which are all logically consistent. To decide which one is true, therefore, we need to appeal to more than reason. We also need to appeal to the evidence of experience. This conclusion fits in with the main rival tradition to rationalism – empiricism.

▶ Empiricism

It sounds like a poor joke, but the adversaries of Descartes, Leibniz and Spinoza were an Englishman, an Irishman and a Scotsman: Locke, Berkeley and Hume. The empiricists rejected the idea that reason alone had the power to understand reality. Instead, they gave the main role in knowledge to experience.

Locke started his great empiricist work, *An Essay Concerning Human Understanding* (1690), by rejecting the then popular theory that the mind contained certain ideas and concepts from birth. We are obviously not aware of these so-called 'innate ideas' from birth, but it was thought we needed them in order to be able to reason.

Locke's critique of innate ideas attempted to show that the mind is a 'clean slate' (or *tabula rasa*) and is furnished by experience, through our five senses. There is no need to postulate the existence of innate ideas since every idea we have can be explained in terms of experience. Locke's argument appeals to a principle known as Ockham's Razor, which states that if there are two competing explanations, then, all other things being equal, one should prefer the one which is simpler. (In Ockham's original version, the principle is strictly that one should prefer the principle which postulates fewer entities.) In Locke's view, it is just a far simpler explanation to suppose we get all our ideas from experience, by mechanisms we can understand and explain, rather than that we get some innately, through mechanisms we can neither know nor explain.

Locke's essay was the first salvo in the empiricist attack on rationalism. By showing how much we depend on experience for our knowledge, it challenged the rationalist view that experience could be set aside when reasoning philosophically. However, one should not think that Locke's idea of the *tabula rasa* is essential to empiricism. David Hume (1711–1776) believed that we were born with not so much ideas, as instincts which shaped our knowledge. For Hume, the mind is not a *tabula rasa*, but is predisposed in certain ways to understand the world. He offered a different challenge to rationalism, one which again put experience over reason.

Hume's main argument was that deductive reason, which the rationalists thought was the route to all knowledge, was actually a very limited instrument. Mathematics, logic and geometry all depended on deductive argument. But knowledge of the world required a different form of reasoning, what we now call induction.

To see the difference, consider first this deductive argument:

All professional athletes are fit.
Angela is a professional athlete.
Therefore, Angela is fit.

In this deductive argument, the conclusion must follow from the premises. If all professional athletes are fit and Angela is a professional athlete, then Angela must be fit.

Now consider this inductive argument:

> There has never been a year without rain in England.
> Therefore, it will rain next year in England.

This argument is different. We may think that the premise provides a good reason to accept the conclusion, but it doesn't necessarily follow from the fact that it has rained every year in England that it will rain next year in England. The possibility, however slight, remains open that next year it won't.

In such an inductive argument we are relying on something other than pure deductive reason to reach our conclusions. These things Hume calls variously custom, habit and experience. What is perhaps surprising is that Hume thought all knowledge of the world was based on this kind of reasoning. We can never prove by deductive reasoning that every event must have a cause, that fire burns or that water quenches thirst. Rather, we learn these things through experience. Further, this learning from experience does not usually take the form of using the evidence of our senses to provide premises for deductive arguments. Reasoning about experience is wholly distinct from deductive reasoning and is therefore not 'rational' in the traditional sense at all.

Empiricism is a pretty radical hypothesis. If true, it shatters the rationalist dream that by reason alone we can discover the ultimate nature of reality and that only one such account of the world will be compatible with reason. If experience is our main guide and experience is not about forming deductive arguments on the basis of the evidence of our senses, then humans are much less rational creatures than the rationalists could ever have imagined.

The main weakness of empiricism is that there do seem to be many truths and principles of thought absolutely essential to good reasoning which are not justified or grounded in experience. The basic rules of logic, for example, are not judged to be true or false on the evidence of the real world. The empiricist needs to explain why they are permitted to help themselves to these intellectual tools while at the same time maintaining that experience provides the grounds for all knowledge.

▶ Foundationalism

Although the rationalists and empiricists were directly opposed to each other in key respects, many of them had in common a commitment to what is sometimes called foundationalism.

The basic idea behind foundationalism is simple. Epistemology is about answering the questions of what and how we can know anything. It is natural to try and answer this by identifying what the basis of our knowledge is. If we can do this and demonstrate that these foundations are secure, then we can build up our knowledge confidently.

The rationalists believed that reason provided the foundations for our knowledge. All that we know is built on the rock of rationality. This rock is secure because, in its essence, reason is ultimately based on nothing more than self-evident truths. The basic principles of good reason are obvious propositions, such as 'nothing can both be and not be at the same time', and simple rules of deduction, such as 'if A and B are true, then B is true'.

The empiricists, on the other hand, believed that the foundations of our knowledge are set in experience. This may not be as immediately reassuring as rationalism, since experience can lead us astray. But by accepting that we have to base our knowledge on the fallible lessons of experience and that reason cannot do all the work, we arguably have a more realistic, attainable foundation for our knowledge.

However, we might question whether the whole foundationalist assumption is a mistake. Building from the bottom up is only one way to construct. Consider an analogy with a wall. One way to build a wall is to build it up, brick by brick, laying the foundations first. This is how foundationalists see knowledge – an intellectual edifice built up from a secure base. However, another way to build a wall is to use four boards to create a mould, fill it with concrete and then remove the boards once the concrete is set. In this way, the wall is created all at once, not from the bottom up. Could this provide a different model for understanding how knowledge is possible?

Over the last two centuries, many philosophers have rejected the foundationalist assumption and have tried to understand knowledge in a different way. They have sought to find pragmatic alternatives to foundationalism

Pragmatism with a capital P is most closely associated with the American philosophers of the late nineteenth and early twentieth centuries, C. S. Peirce, William James and John Dewey. Pragmatism is rooted in a reaction against the correspondence theory of truth, which is an important part of the philosophy of language as well as epistemology.

The correspondence theory understands words (and by extension sentences and the beliefs we have) as standing in a relation to the real world. When our thoughts correspond correctly to the real world, they are true. So, if I have a thought 'the bug is on the rug' and the bug is indeed on the rug, my thought is true. However, if I have the thought which doesn't correspond to the way the world is, such as 'Britain is bigger than America', my thought is false.

The theory sounds like common sense, but it is actually very difficult to give a satisfactory account of what correspondence comprises. One problem is that it seems hard to see what exactly the theory is explaining. What it says is something like this:

'The bug is on the rug' is true if the bug is on the rug.

What is not explained here is how the sentence in inverted commas – 'the bug is on the rug' actually corresponds to the fact of the bug being on the rug. Nor is there any indication here of what the fact corresponding to the sentence is, since the fact is simply the sentence repeated.

For our purposes, we need not dwell on the problems of the correspondence theory. What we need to do is consider the pragmatist alternative. Pragmatism rejected the idea that it is correspondence which makes sentences true. Rather, the truth is what works.

For instance, what makes it true that water freezes at zero degrees centigrade? Rather than say it is because the sentence 'water freezes at zero degrees centigrade' somehow corresponds to a fact or the truth, the pragmatists answer is to say that it is true because taking it to be true allows us to successfully do certain things, such as make ice-cubes or predict on the basis of a thermometer reading whether a water sample will be liquid or solid.

Likewise, 'Britain is bigger than America' is false, not because it fails to correspond, but because one will fail to do anything like plan a journey or make a decent map if one takes it to be true.

Apart from Pragmatism with a capital P, there are many other lower-case pragmatisms. The coherence theory, for instance, says that beliefs are true if they cohere together into a whole system of beliefs which are compatible with experience. Instrumentalism says that beliefs are true if they allow us to do things in the world which we couldn't do unless we took them to be true. All can be called pragmatic theories because they define truth in terms of what works, not in terms of any determinate connection they have with objective facts.

To make the connection between pragmatism and knowledge, one needs to consider the role of truth in knowledge. Remember that at the start of this chapter we said that to know implies that what one knows is true. Foundationalism provides a way to show why what we think we know is true – it is built on solid foundations of experience, rationality or both. On pragmatic conceptions of truth, knowledge does not rest on such foundations. Put crudely, truth is what works, and what works is determined by trial and error, not by building up from secure foundations. Knowledge, which is of what is true, is therefore similarly not foundationalist in nature.

▶ The tripartite account of knowledge

One can see another way in which conceptions of truth plug into conceptions of knowledge by considering one of the most enduring conceptions of what knowledge is – the so-called tripartite account of knowledge. The tripartite account of knowledge has a very noble pedigree. A version of it appears in Platos' dialogue, *Theaetetus*. In it, Socrates and the eponymous interlocutor test out the theory that knowledge is true belief plus a rational account. On this view, knowledge has three parts: a belief, the fact that the belief is true and the fact that one can provide a rational account to show the belief is true.

The modern counterpart of this theory dresses it up in a little jargon. The tripartite account aims to provide the necessary and sufficient conditions for propositional knowledge. By necessary and sufficient conditions, we mean what is required to be the case for something to count as knowledge. By propositional knowledge, we mean something that can be expressed in the form, 'X knows that P', where P is a proposition or sentence. This contrasts with knowledge by acquaintance, which is where I say 'I know X' because I am familiar with it through direct experience. So, 'I know London' is an example of knowledge by acquaintance whereas, 'I know that London is the capital of Britain' is an example of propositional knowledge.

The tripartite account claims that propositional knowledge has three necessary conditions: Justification, truth and belief. Expressed formulaically, this means:

S knows that P if and only if:

1 S believes that P.
2 P is true.
3 S is justified in believing that P.

As we have seen, because 'know' is a success verb, condition (2) must hold. At this point, one may be tempted to ask, 'but how do we know something is true?' This is a legitimate question, but not relevant to the project of providing necessary and sufficient conditions for knowledge. What we are looking for here is not a way of *verifying* whether we do actually know anything or not, but rather what conditions would have to be fulfilled if one were to know something. The question is thus 'what is it to know?', not 'how do we know we know?'

Condition (1) also appears to be necessary. After all, many things are true and justifiable, but if I have no beliefs about them, I cannot know that they are true. This is the *entailment* thesis, that knowledge entails belief or something similar, such as certainty, conviction or acceptance.

However, some hold that there is an *incompatibility* between knowledge and belief, so belief can have no part in knowledge. There are at least three arguments for this.

First, it is claimed that knowledge is by definition infallible. If one knows, one cannot be wrong, as that would simply mean one never knew in the first place. However, belief implies fallibility. Therefore, belief and knowledge are incompatible.

This does not seem to be very persuasive. As belief is only one part of knowledge, there seems no problem in holding that fallible belief plus the other conditions of knowledge add up to infallible knowledge. It's like saying that a bolt can't be part of a mansion, because bolts are cheap and mansions are expensive!

The second argument is that the words have incompatible meanings, illustrated by the familiar protest, 'I don't believe it, I *know* it!' But again, this has an alternative explanation. In such utterances, we are simply pointing out that what we have is not *just* belief, but something more. It doesn't mean belief is not involved. Compare, 'we didn't beat them, we destroyed them!' This means we didn't *just* beat them, we did something more, but still, beating was involved.

The third argument is that since belief entails uncertainty and knowledge entails certainty, knowledge cannot involve belief, as we cannot be both certain and uncertain of the same thing at the same time. However, the premises of this argument are dubious. Some people are certain of their beliefs, even though they cannot be said to know that they are true. Conversely, it doesn't seem impossible for someone to know and yet be uncertain. It is surely possible for there to be two people who believe the same thing to be true with the same justifications. If one just happens to be more confident than the other, it would surely be odd to say that person knows and the other one doesn't. It is unclear that the certainty a person feels has any relevance to whether they know something or not.

This is an interesting point, because there is a tradition in philosophy, found in Plato, for example, of characterising knowledge as if it were a certain special state of mind, of which certainty is one characteristic. On this view, if we could see into people's minds, we would find that knowing is a different mental state to believing, for example. This seems improbable, because whether one knows must surely depend at least partly on what is true of the world. That means that knowing requires something to be true outside of your head as well as in it. So just looking at your state of mind will never be enough to tell us if you know or not – we also need to know what is true of the world.

In addition to the entailment and incompatibility theses, there is the separability thesis. This doesn't go so far as to say that knowledge and belief are incompatible, but it does claim that they can be separated. This would mean that belief cannot be an essential part of knowledge. The idea here is that the test of whether someone knows something is whether they can answer questions correctly about it, whether they can use that knowledge and so on. Now, someone may be able to do these things and yet lack the belief that they know the facts in question. As an example, consider the student who insists they don't know, and the teacher says, 'Yes you do, have a go.' The student then offers what they feel is a guess, and the teacher replies, 'Correct. You see, you did know all along.' This account sounds odd, because one wouldn't normally claim to know something if one didn't believe it and was pretty sure of it. But perhaps there is no contradiction in claiming that one may not be justified in claiming one knows something, even though one does in fact know it. In order for Jack to *say* 'I know', he has to believe and have certainty, but for it to *be true* that 'Jack knows' these conditions may not apply.

The third component of the tripartite account, that the true belief be justified, is probably the most problematic. The main question here is what constitutes justification. People justify their claims to knowledge in all sorts of ways, some good and some bad. However, although this clearly is a thorny issue, it could be said to be irrelevant to the present purposes. We would need to know whether our justification was a good one or not if we are to decide whether we know that P in any particular cases. So, to know that we know we would need to be sure our justification was sound. But we are only concerned here with what is required for knowledge in general. Hence, all we need to consider is whether justification is required, not what *sort* of justification is required. That question can come later.

▶ Against the tripartite account

Many have criticised the tripartite account by showing there are counter-examples where knowledge does not fit the mould of justified true belief. For instance, in D. H. Lawrence's short story, 'The Rocking Horse Winner', a child correctly predicts the winners of horse races time after time. Although there is nothing to justify his beliefs, he is nevertheless right. Hence, we seem to have knowledge without justification. (I owe this example to Michael Proudfoot.)

One reply to this is that this knowledge is justified. It is simply the case that the justification – repeated success – is not available on the earlier occasions. The fact that the justification is temporally after the time of the knowing doesn't mean there is no justification. We cannot *say* that the boy knows until the justification arises, but there is still a justification. The problem with this reply is that had the boy chosen to make just one prediction, then the justification would never have arisen and without the justification the boy could not be said to have known at all. But if the boy knew when he made one prediction which happened to be followed by others, then surely he would have known if he had made the identical prediction but not gone on to make any more. Whether he knows or not surely cannot be determined by what happens after he makes his prediction and the prediction comes true. Whether one knows cannot depend upon facts other than those pertaining to the relationship between fact and knower.

This example presents the possibility of knowledge without one of the three conditions in the tripartite account. Edmund Gettier, however, came up with some counter-examples to show how even if all three conditions are fulfilled, there can still be a lack of knowledge.

In one example, two people, call them Blib and Blob, apply for the same job. Blib justifiably believes that Blob has ten coins in his pocket and that he will get the job. Therefore, by simple logic, he is justified in believing that the person who gets the job has ten coins in his pocket. As it turns out, Blib also has ten coins in his pocket and gets the job. Given that Blib wrongly thought Blob would get the job and didn't know he himself had ten coins in his pocket, it would seem absurd to say he knew that the person who got the job had ten coins in his pocket. Yet he did believe this, his belief was justified and his belief was true. So it seems we have justified true belief without knowledge.

One obvious reply to Gettier is that his examples feature inadequate justifications. The problem here, though, is that if we are to reply to Gettier by specifying what constitutes an adequate justification, we risk either making our requirements so strict that we could never have knowledge, or that further counter-examples will be produced until we do reach these over-strict requirements. For example, if we claim that knowledge requires justification which *guarantees* the truth of the proposition, then at best we would only be able to know necessary truths of logic, definition and mathematics, as no empirical knowledge of the world is justified in such a way as to guarantee it to be true.

Solving Gettier's problems is frustratingly difficult. For instance, one attempt is to add a fourth condition to the three of the tripartite account which specifies the importance of causation, such as:

4   P is the cause of S's belief that P is true.

In the Blib and Blob example above, Blib would not have knowledge because what caused him to have his true justified belief was not the fact that it was true. One objection to this is that it is unclear whether a proposition or fact is the right kind of thing to be a cause of a belief. Facts and propositions do not really cause anything. Another objection comes in the form of a counter-example devised by Alvin Goldman:

> Suppose Sam spots Judy across the street and correctly believes that it is Judy. If it were Judy's twin sister, Trudy, he would mistake her for Judy. Does Sam know that it is Judy? As long as there is serious possibility that the person across the

street might have been Trudy rather than Judy..., we would deny that Sam knows.

(*Epistemology and Cognition*, 1986)

Here, Sam is justified in his true belief that it is Judy, and Judy is the cause of this belief. But he doesn't know it is Judy because there was a large element of luck involved. He would have been just as inclined to say that it was Judy if it had been Trudy, which shows that he doesn't really know who it was – he was just lucky. All three conditions of the tripartite account plus the causal condition are all in play, yet we don't have knowledge.

One odd feature of an enquiry such as this is that when we decide whether or not a set of criteria for knowledge is a good one or not, we seem to already know what counts as knowledge! We confidently assert that Sam doesn't know it is Judy, for example. But how do we know he doesn't know? Because we know what knowledge is and it isn't *that*! We are able to use the concept of knowledge and know when it is applied correctly, and yet every attempt to define it seems to end in failure.

Maybe this is because knowledge is indefinable, or at the very least there are no precise conditions which specify its correct application. It could be a primitive concept; that is to say, a concept so basic that it cannot be defined in yet more simpler terms.

Wittgenstein (1889–1951) would claim that to know what a word means is simply to be able to use it properly, even if we can't precisely define it. Consider the noun 'game'. Games have many different features. Not all involve winning, teams, competition or entertainment, for example. Hence, defining 'game' is very difficult. But someone unable to define what a game is (which is almost all of us) still knows what 'game' means. This is because there is a 'family resemblance' between the various correct usages of 'game' which we come to recognise and this enables us to use the word correctly. If Wittgenstein is right, then we are wrong to think that we need to specify precisely what knowledge is. We know how to use the word 'know' and so already know what knowledge means. It is a kind of philosophical sickness that makes us believe we don't.

▶ Scepticism concerning knowledge

Wittgenstein may provide balm for those who feel philosophy has made us unable to remember what we already knew. But some might think that there is a deeper problem than the failure to answer Gettier's objections. The sceptic says the real problem is that we don't have any knowledge at all, not that we can't define it.

There is an important difference between ordinary scepticism and philosophical scepticism. Ordinary scepticism distinguishes between sources of knowledge which are reliable (such as good science) and unreliable (such as newspaper astrologers). Philosophical scepticism, on the other hand, calls into question the reliability of our system of knowledge in general. In this way, philosophical scepticism is quite indiscriminating. What reasons could we possibly have for accepting such a pessimistic and undermining position?

Many arguments have been advanced for scepticism but as A. J. Ayer (1910–1989) repeatedly pointed out, the basic form of most sceptical arguments is the same. They start by asking what would justify us being certain that any particular belief or proposition was true. They then show that no such justification is possible.

For instance, we might think we would be justified in being certain of statements which are self-evident. Self-evident propositions are those which stand in need of no further justification – they justify themselves. Examples include '2 + 2 = 4', or 'All bachelors are unmarried'.

However, the sceptic can argue that we cannot even be certain of the truth of these statements. In each case, all we are relying on is an intuitive sense that they must be true. But can we trust these intuitions? When we dream, aren't we just as certain about things which we later discover to be manifestly false? Couldn't we be mad people, who are both convinced of the self-evident truth of certain absurdities and totally unaware of their own madness? Could we not have been brainwashed or hypnotised to believe things to be self-evidently true which we would otherwise not accept as such?

The pattern of the sceptic's argument is the same when she turns her attention to the basis of our beliefs in sense experience, as we shall see soon. By showing that there are no certain foundations to our knowledge, the sceptic makes the whole possibility of knowledge problematic, if not impossible.

The sceptic follows the same line when considering how we use reason to give us knowledge of the world. The sceptic, following Hume, starts by observing that all reasoning about the world is inductive in form (see the section on empiricism above). But inductive reasoning, as we have seen, does not guarantee the truth of its conclusions. That means we can never be certain that what we have concluded from a piece of inductive reasoning is true, so again we have cast doubt on the possibility of our having knowledge.

Put these three strands of scepticism together and it seems we have no knowledge at all. We cannot be certain that self-evident statements are true. We cannot be certain that what we perceive exists. We cannot be certain that the conclusions of our reasoning about the world are true. In short, we cannot be certain of anything.

Scepticism is not short of critics. Gilbert Ryle (1900–1976), for example, argues that the sceptic robs the idea of 'certain knowledge' of any meaning by insisting that it doesn't exist. He uses the analogy that the concept of false coins only makes sense if there are genuine ones. The philosophical sceptic, however, labels all our supposed knowledge as 'false coins', which would seem to make no sense if there is no true knowledge for it to contrast with. Ignorance implies knowledge, so by denying we have any knowledge the sceptic robs the idea of ignorance of any content.

In reply to this, it could be argued that scepticism is not the claim that nothing is true, it is rather the claim that we cannot distinguish truth and falsehood. This means that, as far as we are concerned, we can never be sure that we have knowledge. But the objection could still hold. Returning to the coins analogy, if there is no possible means of distinguishing between false and true coins, isn't the distinction meaningless?

This discussion reinforces the point made earlier about the difference between ordinary and philosophical scepticism. The philosophical scepticism I have outlined is not justified by experience. A scientist may cast doubt on a theory by citing other empirical evidence, but the sceptic cannot cast doubt on the existence of the world itself by citing empirical evidence. The sceptic considers what empirical evidence can and can't do, not whether any particular piece of empirical evidence casts doubt on our knowledge. The sceptic's general doubt makes all evidence suspect, not only in cases where we appear to be deluded. In essence, then, the sceptic does not base her argument on experience, but bases it on the hypothesis that our standards of proof are logically defective.

At the root of the sceptic's doubts lies the quest for certainty and the conviction that such certainty cannot be attained. The quest for certainty has been seen as a fundamental part of the theory of knowledge, the idea being that without certainty, we cannot have knowledge. Thus, it appears the sceptic only needs to remove certainty to remove our claim to knowledge. It is this which seems to make scepticism inevitable. As Ayer says: 'There can be doubt so long as there is the possibility of error.'

Perhaps this is the problem. There are many different concepts all getting tangled up in the sceptic's web. First, there is knowledge, which is about a relation the knower has to information or facts. Then there is certainty, which in its primary usage is about a state of mind. (We can say 'it is certain' rather than 'I am certain' and thus not refer to a state of mind, but this is another usage of certain.) Next there is doubt, which is also a psychological state.

The point is that certainty, knowledge and doubt are all distinct. It does not seem to be self-contradictory, for example, to say that I know something, even though I'm not certain of it. Similarly, I can be certain of something and yet not know it, since I am in fact wrong. Could it, then, be that in tying the idea of certainty and immunity from doubt so closely to the idea of knowledge, the sceptic – and those she attacks – have made a fundamental mistake?

It is also possible to rebuke the sceptic by rejecting the foundationalist approach to knowledge (see the section on foundationalism above). Scepticism works by undermining the foundations of our knowledge. But if we accept a pragmatic, coherence or instrumentalist conception of knowledge, then perhaps we can sidestep the sceptic's challenge. If our knowledge has no foundations to undermine, then the sceptic's attack leaves no sting.

▶ Scepticism concerning perception

Scepticism has perhaps been most influential in arguments concerning perception. The sceptic's prime target here is naïve realism. Naïve realism is the view that the world is more or less as we perceive it to be. This view is threatened by the widely held idea that we do not perceive the world directly. If this is true, then there may be sceptical repercussions. It may be that we don't perceive the external world at all, or it could even be true that there is no external world.

Many philosophers have, in fact, concluded that we do not perceive the world directly. It is rather that we have perceptions, and from these perceptions we infer the existence of the external world. That which we perceive have variously been called ideas (Locke, Berkeley), impressions (Hume) or sense data (Russell, Moore).

Sense data are not things in the mind which have been discovered by science. There is no experimental way of distinguishing between seeing an object and seeing a sense datum. So why then introduce sense data? The most popular argument for sense data is the argument from illusion, one primitive version of which is:

When I look at a distant house, what I see is small.
The house is not small.
Therefore, what I see is not a house.

This is clearly unsound, as it begs the question to say that what I see *is* small. Surely, all I can say is that it *appears* small. If the first premise is thus amended, the argument then becomes invalid, unless we add a third premise which states: 'If X has the property a, and Y appears to have a property incompatible with a, then X cannot be Y.' However, it is far from clear why we should accept this as a premise.

Similar objections can be raised against this subtler version of the argument:

We often perceive something not as it really is.
In such cases, we are perceiving something.
Therefore, it cannot be the object itself we are perceiving.
Therefore, we must be perceiving something else, i.e. sense data.

We can take this one stage further and argue that we always see sense data. If it is true that in such cases when we perceive something not as it really is that we perceive sense data, and there is nothing to distinguish such perceptual experiences from veridical perceptions, then it would seem that we always perceive sense data. It would be very odd if perception sometimes were of sense data and sometimes of the object itself, even though the experience was identical in both cases.

Unfortunately, this argument is also flawed. The argument is only valid if we accept the rulings, 'in every case where an object seems to be perceived there is something directly perceived,' (which is required for the second premise to be true) and 'that which is directly perceived cannot appear otherwise than as it is' (which is required for the first conclusion to follow).

In the first case, it is not clear that we can give any sense to the idea of direct perception unless we can contrast it with indirect perception. If it is true that ordinary perception of objects is indirect, then what would it mean to perceive them directly? The problem is that perception is always, in some sense, indirect. The whole point about perception is that it is awareness of an object through the medium of one or more senses. This is as direct as perception can ever get. It may make sense to talk about perception via a reflection or television, for example, as being indirect. But to talk about ordinary perception as being indirect as opposed to direct seems to be making a contrast with something that doesn't exist.

As for the second ruling – 'that which is directly perceived cannot appear otherwise than as it is' – there just seems to be no good reason to accept it. Extraordinary though it may seem, many philosophers seem to have assumed that something like this must be true. If I see a castle through a heat haze, for instance, it seems perfectly acceptable to say I am directly perceiving the castle, yet it is not appearing as it really is, since it isn't actually shimmering. There just seems no good reason to deny this possibility.

A further version of the argument for sense data is:

Every time I see an X, it is possible that X may not be there.
So I should say, 'I seem to see an X'.
This can also be phrased as 'I see a seeming X'.
This seeming X is a sense datum.

For example, did Macbeth see a dagger? Well, he seemed to see a dagger, so we could say he saw a seeming dagger, that is a sense datum of a dagger. But this could be dismissed as unnecessary 'reification'. Reification is the process of taking a phenomenon to be a certain kind of object. In this case, we are taking the phenomenon of 'seeming to see a dagger' and creating an object 'a seeming dagger'. But to seem to see an X is not the same as to see a seeming X, as the latter supposes that there is something there to be seen, whereas the former does not. We could equally say of Macbeth that he saw nothing, or thought he saw a dagger. The point is that to have a visual experience does not entail that there is something which one is seeing.

Ryle makes this objection even more convincing when he talks of the sense data theorist making a 'logical howler'; namely, 'assimilating the concept of sensation to the concept of observation'. With observation, the thing observed is not immediate to the observer. For example, one can have a good or bad view of what one is observing, one's observation can be more or less clear or striking. These things are not true of sensations. Sensations are immediate to the person having the sensation. One does not introspect to *observe* one's pain, one simply *has* the pain.

Ryle argues that the having of a perception is more like a sensation than an observation. It cannot be a form of observation for the following reason: perception requires the object perceived and the perception of that object. If having a perception is like an observation, then the perception itself must be observed or perceived. We would then have the perception and the perception of the perception. But then the perception of the perception would also have to be observed, so we would need a perception of the perception of the perception, and so on. To prevent this infinite regress (a never ending requirement for the perception to be perceived), we have to conclude that a perception cannot itself be perceived or observed.

The upshot is that we should think of a perception as more like a sensation which is simply 'had' than an observation of sense data. This removes the regress. But then the sense data model would have to be rejected, as this model assumes that in perception, it is sense data that are directly perceived, which follows the observation model.

A. J. Ayer has a good reply to this objection. He claims that there is no general principle that the having of a perception itself entails a further perception. It is simply that in the particular case of perceiving physical objects, we have grounds for believing it is not the objects themselves which are perceived.

Who is right? There is no consensus on this debate. If Ayer is right, then we do not perceive the world directly, and the world may well be very different to the way it appears. Hence, naïve realism would be defeated. But if Ryle is correct, that wouldn't necessarily mean naïve realism triumphed. There are other competing models for perception.

Ryle's view is compatible with the causal theory of perception, which states that:

1 Objects have those properties which science indicates that they have.
2 Perceived qualities are caused by these actual properties interacting with the environment and the observer.

This seems compatible with a weak form of naïve realism, which simply claims that objects are directly perceived. Although the physical properties causing perception are not themselves perceived, nevertheless, the object itself is the direct cause of our perceptions, and so in a sense objects are directly perceived. There is nothing between the perceiver and object as there is in the sense data theory.

Although the scientific view which informs the causal theory is arguably itself based on observations of sense data, the fact that science explains and predicts so well gives us good reasons to believe our scientific view is correct.

One potentially serious difficulty for this view is that it still creates a huge chasm between the world as it is and the world as it is actually perceived. The world appears as a collection of solid, coloured, textured objects, not a seething mass of colourless particles in motion. It appears then, that no strong form of naïve realism can really be compatible with this view. Yet part of the appeal of the causal theory is that it seems to be based on a scientific realism which is the natural successor to naïve realism. But if scientific realism is true, surely naïve realism is false. The world just isn't as it appears.

On the other hand, it could be said that scientific realism is compatible with naïve realism. Just because science says a table is a collection of molecules, does that mean that the table isn't 'really' hard, brown, square and so on? Possibly not. Science is concerned with micro-properties, whereas hardness, shape and so on are macro-properties, not there on the molecular level but certainly real on the macro level. After all, what does it mean to say the table is not 'really' brown? This makes sense if we mean that it is in odd light, for example, or that it has been painted over. To say it is not really brown is to suggest it has a real colour or no colour at all. The scientific view does not suggest either. As colour is something only evident to those who perceive an object, what science says about an object's deep structure cannot have any bearing on whether it really has colour or not.

We are beginning to move away from the centre of epistemology and into metaphysics, which considers questions surrounding the fundamental nature of reality. Epistemology and metaphysics are very closely related and many universities offer classes in both, nicknamed 'ep and met'. To conclude this chapter, we will look at three major metaphysical positions – realism, idealism and phenomenalism – and see how they tie in with epistemological arguments.

▶ Realism

Realism is simply the view that objects exist independently of our perceptions of them. An optimistic realist would say that we also are able to know about the nature of this real world. The sceptic, on the other hand, accepts the existence of the real world but denies we can have knowledge of it. Thus, the assumption of realism is required for both the most optimistic and pessimistic accounts of our possibilities for knowledge.

Realism is a common-sense view and one tends not to see many positive arguments for it. Rather, people defend realism by arguing against rival positions, such as idealism and phenomenalism. So, much of what can be said about realism will be covered in what is said against idealism and phenomenalism.

One example of a positive argument for realism comes from John Searle (see his *Mind, Language and Society*). He offers a kind of transcendental argument. A transcendental argument starts from what we know to be true in experience and then goes on to show what must be the case in order for this to be true.

In Searle's argument, the starting point is that ordinary discourse is meaningful and allows us to do certain things. For instance, if we arrange to meet up at a certain time and place, then assuming we have accurate watches, maps and so on, we will do so. None of this makes sense, argues Searle, unless we make the assumption that 'there is a place, in space in time, that is independent of us and we can meet at that particular place.' That assumption is precisely what realism is.

Realism is obviously very attractive, even though it creates space for the sceptic. However, it faces many challenges, the most illustrious of which is idealism.

▶ Idealism

The empiricist philosopher John Locke (1632–1704) distinguished between the primary and secondary qualities of objects. Primary qualities are those of size, shape, solidity, number and motion. These were thought to be properties objects had regardless of whether anyone was observing them or not. Secondary qualities, however, depend upon the perceiver. Colour, texture and temperature, for instance, all vary according to the nature of the perceiver. The colour of what we call a red ball, for instance, looks very different to a normally sighted person, to someone who is colour-blind or to a dog. The same water feels tepid if your hand is cold, yet cold if your hand is hot. A surface smooth for a human can be a rough, rugged landscape for an ant.

Locke's view was essentially a realist one. He thought that primary qualities were the real properties of objects and that these existed independently of any minds. Secondary qualities accounted for the fact that objects may appear differently to us but they do not cast doubt on the basic independent reality of things.

However, Bishop George Berkeley (1685–1753) disagreed, and turned Locke's arguments against him to support a decidedly non-realist alternative. Berkeley contended that, to be consistent, Locke should have acknowledged that what he called primary qualities were really secondary qualities. Consider shape. In what way can we talk about shape independently from sense experience? If a box is square, that is because it looks and feels square. Take away the idea of look and feel from the idea of square and what are you left with? Nothing, contends Berkeley. That means you need sense perception to have the idea of an object's shape, so the idea that shape is a primary quality which exists independently of sense perception doesn't make sense. Shape, therefore, has to be a secondary quality, like colour and taste.

Berkeley said similar things about the other so-called primary qualities. The root of his argument is that all properties of an object are only known to us through sense perception. They are all thus sense dependent, not sense independent.

This view has a remarkable upshot. If all the properties of an object are sense dependent, and an object is after all no more than the sum of all its properties, then that must mean that all objects are sense dependent. Realism is thus false. Objects do not exist whether they are perceived or not. Objects only exist because they are perceived. As Berkeley put it, their *esse* is *percipi* – to be is to be perceived.

This thesis is known as idealism, so called because things which are perceived are ideas in some mind, rather than material objects in a mind-independent world. If true, it raises some odd questions. For instance, if objects only exist as ideas in minds, what happens if I leave an empty, windowless room and shut the door? With no-one there to perceive the objects in it, do they no longer exist? Berkeley thought that would indeed be true, but mindful of its absurdity, perhaps, he concluded that because the mind of God is all-perceiving, objects continue to exist at all times because God perceives them all.

The main weakness of Berkeley's view, as Bertrand Russell pointed out, is that it seems to misunderstand what it means for something to be in a mind. If I think about someone, there is a sense in which I have that person 'in mind'. Indeed, they have to be in my mind in some sense for me to think about them. But, obviously, that doesn't mean the actual person is walking around in my head.

In a similar way, when I perceive an object, I need certain ideas to be in my head. I need to have an idea of its shape, texture, colour and so on. But that doesn't necessarily mean that the shape, texture and colour themselves are actually in my head. It is a simple truism to say that to know an object I need to have mental ideas of that object. But it doesn't follow from this that the object is nothing more than these ideas.

Despite its intuitive implausibility, idealism has continued to be a theory with many supporters. It also has a distinguished cousin, which it is sometimes confused with: phenomenalism.

▶ Phenomenalism

Phenomenalism has a different starting point to idealism; namely, the acceptance that there are sense data. However, it tries to avoid the scepticism that sense data can introduce when it seems that sense data stand between us and a direct perception of the real world. It does this by claiming that sense data do not stand between us and objects because talk of objects is no more than talk of sense data. The phenomenalist thesis is that physical objects are logical constructs out of sense data. Mill put it by saying that objects were 'permanent possibilities of sensation'. All talk of objects, according to the phenomenalist, is reducible to talk about sense data. So, for example, everything I say about my house can be reduced to statements about sense data. There is no further reference to an object beyond those sense data.

Consider, for example, 'ice-cream'. Once you add up all the sense data associated with ice-cream – its texture, consistency, flavour, smell, colour, temperature and so on – you have actually said all there is to say about it. You don't need to add 'and all these sense-data correspond to an object which we call ice-cream'. The object just is all those sense data.

An obvious objection to this theory is that it is in the very idea of an object that it can exist unperceived. Therefore, it cannot be true that all talk about sense-independent objects can be reduced to talk of sense-dependent experience. The phenomenalist would reply that, on their view, objects can exist unperceived. All they insist on is a hypothetical clause, so that to say X exists is to say that, under the right circumstances, the appropriate sense data would occur. The idea of an object that would never produce any sense data is, on their view, meaningless.

Note that phenomenalism is thus a logical thesis about what it means for something to exist. Idealism, though closely related, is an ontological thesis, as it is about the nature of things which exist. Phenomenalism merely claims talk of objects is a logical construct of sense data – it doesn't deny that objects exist. This is a simple, fundamental and important difference and one worth getting clear about to avoid confusing idealism and phenomenalism.

The introduction of the hypothetical clause doesn't seem convincing. As Isaiah Berlin said, the existence of objects is not hypothetical but categorical. To say something exists is to say it exists, full stop, not that it would exist if perceived. The implausibility of phenomenalism is that it claims categorical talk of public objects is a construct of hypothetical talk about private experience.

There may also be a regress in the phenomenalist thesis. If to exist is to be observed, we need an observer. But if the observer is to exist, then she also needs to be observed. Then you would need another observer, and so on, *ad infinitum*.

There are two other swift and incisive objections against phenomenalism. First, as the having of a sense datum does not logically entail that the object exists (think of hallucinations, etc.), it is clear that statements about objects cannot be just logical constructs of sense data. Second, the existence of an object does not logically entail that a sense datum must occur. Thus, there is a clear logical independence of sense data and objects.

▶ Conclusion

Epistemology attempts to answer questions such as 'how can we have knowledge?' As we have seen, these are very tricky questions to answer. Much depends on how high a standard for knowledge we set. If knowledge requires certainty, perhaps it is unattainable. If knowledge must be of reality independent of experience, maybe we can never have it, since all experience is mediated by experience. If knowledge requires a secure foundation, then maybe we can never have it, because no foundations are firm enough.

Whenever we are faced with a pessimistic option, however, there is usually a more optimistic, though perhaps less ambitious alternative. Maybe knowledge requires something less than certainty. Maybe we don't need to reach a world independent of sense experience to gain knowledge. Maybe knowledge doesn't build from the bottom up.

The choices we make when navigating through epistemology require us to strike a balance between setting the standard for knowledge so low that any old belief counts as knowledge, or setting the standard so high that we find it is unattainable. Getting the right attitude to knowledge therefore requires something more than just sound philosophical reasoning. It requires good judgement. Perhaps we might even call it wisdom.

Summary

The theory of knowledge is concerned with questions of the basis and justification of knowledge. Rationalists have argued that all knowledge is founded on reason, which does not need to appeal to the evidence of experience to demonstrate truths. Empiricists, in contrast, believe all knowledge drives from experience and that only truths of logic, geometry and mathematics can be known to be true without reference to experience. Both empiricism and rationalism can be seen as foundationalist, in that they attempt to discover what the foundation of knowledge is and build up from there.

An alternative to foundationalism is pragmatism, which defines knowledge and truth in terms of what works, without demanding a secure basis for this knowledge.

One of the most important definitions of knowledge is justified true belief – the so-called tripartite account of knowledge. On this view, to know something is to believe something which is true and to be justified in this belief. There are several objections to this. Although some think that knowledge entails belief, others think that knowledge and belief are incompatible, since knowledge has features belief does not. There are also counter-examples where people seem to have knowledge without one of the components of the tripartite account, or where all three components are in place but we don't seem to have knowledge.

An alternative to the tripartite account is to take a Wittgensteinian approach, which claims that the meaning of 'know' is given by the way the word is used and just cannot be specified in a formulaic definition.

Sceptical arguments attempt to show that we do not have any knowledge at all. They work by claiming that certainty is required for knowledge and then showing that such certainty cannot be attained. Sceptics can claim we cannot be certain that self-evident statements are true, that what we perceive exists or that our reasoning is sound. Sceptical arguments concerning the existence of objects include the argument from illusion and more general arguments from sense data. Critics say that sceptics set an impossible standard for knowledge and that by making knowledge impossible they make meaningless the concept of ignorance.

Metaphysical views relate to the theory of knowledge. Realism is the view that objects exist independently of our experience. Optimistic realists believe we can know this reality; pessimistic realists are sceptics. Idealism is the view that everything which exists is mental in nature. Phenomenalism is the view that all talk of objects is really talk of sense data.

Glossary

Coherence theory   The theory that a proposition is true if it coheres (or fits in with) other true beliefs.

Correspondence theory   The theory that propositions are true if they correspond to reality.

Entailment thesis   The idea that knowledge requires belief, in contrast to the views that knowledge can be separated from belief or that knowledge is incompatible with belief.

Epistemic   The adjective, meaning 'concerning knowledge'.

Epistemology   The technical name for the theory of knowledge.

Innate ideas   Ideas we are born with rather than learn from experience.

Propositional knowledge   Knowledge of truths which can be expressed in statements or propositions; that is to know that something is the case.

Qualities   Primary qualities belong to the objects themselves. Secondary qualities only exist in our perceptions of objects.

Self-evident truths   Truths which do not require any further justification.

Sense data   Perceptions, which are arguably all we are directly aware of.

Transcendental argument   An argument that starts from an experience we cannot deny we have and attempts to show what must be true for that experience to be possible.

Further reading

In the companion volume to his book, *Philosophy: Key Texts*, I look at three books which focus on epistemology: Descartes's *Meditations*, Hume's *An Enquiry concerning Human Understanding* and Russell's *The Problems of Philosophy*. All three of these can be read with care by a novice as well as by experts.

Other accessible twentieth-century texts include *The Problem of Knowledge* by A. J. Ayer (Penguin) and *The View from Nowhere* by Thomas Nagel (Oxford University Press), both of which address the challenges of scepticism. Other classic texts worth reading include Berkeley's *The Principles of Human Knowledge*, which is the classic exposition of idealism, and Plato's *Theaetetus*, an instructive run through some early theories of knowledge.

A Companion to Epistemology, edited by Jonathan Dancy and Ernest Sosa (Blackwell) is an excellent reference book with entries long enough to be read as mini-essays. It is too detailed for the casual reader, but highly recommended for anyone seriously studying epistemology.

2 Moral Philosophy

▶ What is moral philosophy?

Unlike many branches of philosophy, it is quite easy to express clearly the main question of ethics, or moral philosophy. It is found in the title of books on the subject, such as *How Should One Live?* by Roger Crisp and *How Are We to Live?* by Peter Singer. But, as ever, things are not quite as simple as they appear. This apparently simple question contains a concept which is highly problematic: 'should' or 'ought'.

As any parent knows, when you say someone *should* or *ought* to do something, that is often not the end of the matter but the beginning. The problem is that the status of this 'ought' is not clear. Is it an absolute command or is it in some way conditional?

Consider the first possibility. One might argue that when one says 'you ought to tell the truth', for example, the question 'why?' doesn't arise. You ought not to lie just because that is one of the things you ought not to do. Moral 'oughts' like this are simple, absolute commands. We follow them because morality demands that they be followed.

But this is an unsatisfactory response. When a parent tells their child they shouldn't hurt other children, for example, and the child asks why, it seems inadequate to reply by saying it is just wrong. It does not seem unreasonable to want to know why this moral rule should be followed. At the very least, we need to know why this is a moral rule at all, rather than just a piece of advice like, 'you ought to see the new Spielberg film'.

To offer an explanation of why we ought to do certain things is to make 'ought' somehow conditional. By that, I mean that every sentence of the form 'You ought to do X' is really a kind of shorthand for a sentence of the form, 'If you want Y, you ought to do X'. An example from moral philosophy should make this clear.

Consider the person who thinks morality is just what God commands. (This is known as the divine command theory.) On this view, to say, 'You ought to obey the Ten Commandments' is to say, 'If you want to obey God's will, you ought to obey the Ten Commandments'. You could, of course, ask why you ought to obey

God's will, and the reason for this might be something like, 'You won't get to heaven if you don't' or 'God knows what's best for us'. This would mean an even more complete unpacking of the simple 'ought' sentence would be, 'If you want to get to heaven, you ought to obey the Ten Commandments' or 'If you want what's best for you, you ought to obey the Ten Commandments'.

Other moral theories will imply similar conditional statements. Utilitarianism, for instance, is the view that it is right to increase happiness and reduce suffering, and wrong to do the opposite. So if a utilitarian says, 'You ought not to hit people unprovoked,' what they really mean is 'If you want to increase happiness and reduce suffering, you ought not to hit people unprovoked'.

You may well have already noticed that this approach has its own problems. It is always possible to ask why one should want what follows the 'if' in such a sentence. Why should I want to get to heaven? Why should I want to reduce suffering and increase happiness? Why should I want what's best for me? When one asks a question like this, one is really looking at the basis for morality and asking why one should be moral at all. Here, it seems the 'ought' or 'should' cannot be justified any further. If we can't see why we ought to want to go to heaven, increase happiness or do what's best for ourselves, then we have some kind of moral blindness.

This touches on some fundamental issues of moral philosophy. First, there is the question of what the foundation of morality really is. Is it, for instance, just a way of getting to heaven, of increasing happiness on earth, or of serving our own self-interests? Second, there is the question of why we ought to be moral at all. At some stage it seems we have to confront the basic choice of whether to be moral or not. If someone rejects morality, have they done wrong? We may think someone is rash or foolish to reject their way into heaven or refuse to do what's best for them. We may despise the person who doesn't care for human happiness. But if we can't say why they ought to have chosen differently, can we condemn them?

As we can see, then, though it may be a simple matter to say moral philosophy is about how we ought to live, there is nothing at all simple about explaining what this 'ought' means.

▶ The divisions of moral philosophy

Moral philosophy can be divided into three main levels of enquiry. At its most practical, it is about what we ought to do in any given situation. This we can call the level of applied ethics. Most ethical discussions in the media are conducted at this level and include questions such as: Is it ever right to clone a human being? Is euthanasia morally wrong? Can we justify our treatment of farmed animals?

To answer such questions, one often needs to go up a level and consider general theories about what the right or wrong thing to do is. This takes us to the level of normative ethics, where we find general theories about what kinds of things are right or wrong. So, for example, a normative ethical theory might say that it is always wrong to kill any creature that has the capacity to decide its own future and has not chosen to be killed. This is not a theory about which *particular* things are right or wrong, but what *kinds* of things are right or wrong. Someone working at the level of applied ethics who agreed with this normative ethic would then try and see what implications this rule has for specific issues, such as those of cloning, euthanasia and animal welfare.

However, the debate can go up another level again to what is called 'meta-ethics', which deals with the status of moral claims in general. For instance, when someone says it is wrong to kill any creature that has the capacity to decide its own future and has not chosen to be killed, what kind of claim are they making? Are they saying something that is true or false, or are they just expressing an opinion? Are they saying something which applies to everyone, or only to people from a particular culture or historical period? What is the basis of what they say? Is morality rooted in nature, human nature, God, or do we just create it ourselves? These are issues of meta-ethics. They are about the general nature and structure of ethics rather than what kinds of actions are right or wrong.

We could see meta-ethics, normative ethics and applied ethics as three levels of enquiry in moral philosophy. Alternatively, we could see them as describing three general areas on a continuum, running from the most specific questions of what we are to do, to the most general questions about the nature of ethics. The advantage of this way of looking at it is that it is almost always impossible to discuss ethics purely at one level. For example, when discussing the meta-ethical issue of whether moral principles are just opinions, examples from applied ethics – such as the fact that torture is wrong – are often invoked to criticise such a view. Like much in moral philosophy, the labels we apply here do not describe things which are entirely distinct but general areas which merge into each other.

My approach here will be to start from the top down, first looking at issues in meta-ethics, then normative ethics and, finally, some issues in applied ethics.

▶ Morality and realism

A fundamental question about the nature of ethics concerns whether or not moral values are real. In one sense, of course, they must be real since people hold them. The philosophical issue of moral realism, however, is the more specific one of whether or not moral values are independent from the people who hold them. Perhaps the easiest way to understand this is by an analogy with art.

When someone looks at, for example, Michelangelo's sculpture of David and says that it is beautiful, what do they mean? They could mean that there is some fact of the matter, that the sculpture is or is not beautiful and that they believe it is true to say that it is. On this view, beauty is a real quality of the sculpture and one can be right or wrong when one claims that the sculpture is or is not beautiful. On the other hand, they might think that they are merely expressing an opinion when they say it is beautiful. On this view, beauty is in the eye of the beholder. If two people disagree about whether the sculpture is beautiful, it is not the case that one of them must be wrong. Rather, both have their opinions and that's all there is to say on the matter. On this view, beauty is not a real property of the sculpture, but a value judgement we each as individuals make.

The same kind of distinction can be made in ethics. When I say 'causing animals to suffer needlessly' is wrong, I could mean one of two things. I could mean that wrongness is a real quality of causing such suffering and one can be right or wrong when one claims that causing such suffering is wrong. On the other hand, I could mean that I am merely expressing an opinion when I say causing such suffering is wrong. On this view, morality is in the eye of the beholder. If you think causing such suffering is not wrong, it is not the case that one of us is making a mistake. Rather, we both have our opinions and that's all there is to say on the matter.

Those who think there are facts about right and wrong are known as moral realists. If, in addition, they believe that such facts can be known by us, they are known as cognitivists. Those who think there are no such facts about right and wrong are called non-realists, and since this means they do not think there is anything one can know about such facts (since they don't exist) they are also known as non-cognitivists. Non-cognitivism is perhaps best captured in the words of Shakespeare's Hamlet: 'There is nothing either good or bad, but thinking makes it so' (Act 2, Scene 2).

Historically, moral realism has been by far the more popular of the two theories. Indeed, it can appear to be quite shocking to deny that moral judgements are correct or incorrect. When we say that torture is wrong, for example, we do not generally think we are merely expressing an opinion. We think torture just is wrong, fact. So why have versions of non-cognitivism proved to be so popular in modern philosophy?

▶ Non-cognitivism

One reason why non-cognitivism can be appealing is that, when we look at other cultures, we find that people hold very different moral views. For instance, while it is perfectly acceptable to charge interest on loans in Christian countries, such a practice is contrary to Islamic ethics. While polygamy is considered morally wrong in most Western countries, there are communities there and in other parts of the world where it is perfectly acceptable. If we hold the cognitivist view, it seems we are forced to say that some of these countries or communities are behaving immorally while some are behaving well. This smacks of Western imperialism. Who are we to say that people with different cultures than our own are wrong? Isn't that both arrogant and intolerant? Non-cognitivism provides a way out, since its implication seems to be that we should not judge other cultures by our own standards. Morality is in the eye (or the culture) of the beholder, it is not some independent thing which applies to everyone.

However, the view that non-cognitivism is the only route to tolerance is highly questionable. First, tolerance could well be a value in the one true ethical system. The mere possibility of that means there is no necessary link between tolerance and non-cognitivism.

Second, if morality is not universal, then that does not mean that the values we choose must include tolerance. We might think that there is no fact of the matter as to whether our ethics are right and someone else's are wrong, but that's not going to stop us fighting tooth and nail for our own values.

Valuing tolerance, then, is not a good enough reason to be a non-cognitivist. Better reasons are offered by thinking about what could make moral claims right or wrong. Compare ethical claims to ordinary, factual claims. If I say 'water freezes at zero degrees centigrade', there are ways of seeing if this is true, which involve going out and seeing if water does in fact freeze at this temperature. If I say 'the square root of 289 is 17', I can see if this is true by standard mathematical procedures. But how can I go about seeing if 'smacking children is wrong' is true? I cannot examine examples of such smacking to see if I can observe the wrongness. Nor can I prove it is wrong in the way in which I can prove a mathematical sum. It is no use conducting an opinion poll because that will only tell me what people *think* is wrong, not what *is* wrong. In short, it seems that whatever moral claims are, they are not the same kinds of things as facts. And if they are not facts, they cannot be true or false.

None the less, we do say things are right or wrong. What do we mean by this if there are no moral facts? A non-cognitivist might answer that when a person says that something is morally good or bad, she is simply approving or disapproving of it. At its most extreme, this view was manifest in a theory called emotivism. On this view, moral statements are expressions of feeling which are neither right nor wrong. They can be compared to statements like 'Ugh! Not gooseberries!', which express reactions but cannot be said to be right or wrong. Ejaculations like 'ugh!' and 'hurrah!' are neither true nor false. On this view, moral error is impossible and moral disagreement futile. Just as it literally makes no sense to say 'you should like Gooseberries' or 'I was wrong when I didn't like peas', it does not make sense to make such statements about moral principles.

There are, however, several problems with this conception of ethics. First, it is possible to distinguish between what I dislike or disapprove of and what I think is morally wrong. For instance, I might approve of someone brutally murdering someone who tortures my family, even though on reflection I cannot morally justify it. Similarly, I might be disgusted by the idea of my grandmother marrying a 20-year-old without thinking her decision is morally wrong. But if morality just is an expression of what I approve of or like, such distinctions would be impossible.

▶ The role of reason

Perhaps the greatest problem for non-cognitivism is that it seems to leave no room at all for reason and reflection. For example, non-cognitivism entails that moral error is impossible, since moral judgements are neither true nor false. One reason why this is a problem is that when we change our minds about moral issues, it often (but by no means always) is precisely because of rational reflection. People came to see that black slavery is wrong at least partly because they came to realise that there was no rational justification for the different treatment of people of different skin colour. Many people are troubled by the morality of abortion because they cannot see any rational principle that would draw a sharp dividing line between the early foetus and the new-born child. In both cases, when people change their minds about their moral stances, they see their previous one as being mistaken. But if non-cognitivism were true, it would not be possible to say that we used to hold incorrect moral principles.

This highlights the fact that reason does play a role in ethics. Although it is true that offering reasons why we don't like gooseberries is a fairly pointless activity, anyone who said that all students are evil and didn't offer a reason for this claim would be thought to be a little crazy.

As it is clear that thinking things through does change our moral principles, and that this process of thinking through actually seems to be central to good ethics, it seems that any credible non-cognitivist theory must find a place for rationality. Prescriptivism is one attempt to do just this.

▶ Prescriptivism

Prescriptivism is a fairly recent moral theory, most closely associated with the work of Richard Hare. Prescriptivism has two key characteristics, one negative, one positive. The positive is that it views moral judgements as prescribing courses of actions. This means that if one accepts a moral judgement and can act upon it, one does so act. For example, consider the moral judgement, 'It is wrong to steal'. If one accepts this is true, then this judgement prescribes a course of action – not stealing. And if one genuinely accepts this moral judgement, one will not, in fact, steal. Prescriptivism is thus an *internalist* doctrine. That is to say, it claims that to make a moral judgement sincerely is to commit oneself to the action specified in the judgement, or to will that someone else do it.

The negative part is that moral judgements are not descriptive and can never be entailed by anything merely descriptive. A descriptive statement contrasts with a prescriptive one in that descriptive statements set out facts and can be true or false, whereas prescriptive statements set out a course of action and cannot be true or false. The command to do something can be obeyed or disobeyed, but it cannot be true or false.

Why can't prescriptive judgments be derived from descriptive ones? The answer is explained in terms of the so-called is/ought gap, which Hume discusses in his *Enquiry concerning the Principles of Morals* (1751). Hume pointed out that many people make the mistake in ethics of starting off talking about facts – things which *are* – and then talking about value – what *should be*. But they do so without justifying this shift from 'is' to 'ought'.

Hume's point is essentially a logical one. In a deductive argument, one can never derive a conclusion which contains an 'ought' unless there is at least one 'ought' in the premises. This 'ought' can be implied, but it has to be there somewhere. Consider this example:

Fare-dodging on the train is the equivalent of theft.
Theft is wrong.
Therefore, one ought not fare-dodge.

Here, the argument is not strictly valid. The conclusion only follows if we add the premise:

One ought not to do what is wrong.

Of course, many people would say that this premise is implied by the premise 'Theft is wrong'. But it is important to realise that strictly speaking, the conclusion 'Therefore one should not fare-dodge' does not follow without it. Without this premise, one cannot get from the purely descriptive premises to the prescriptive conclusion.

To make this clearer, consider this argument.

Torture causes great pain.
Sleep deprivation is a form of torture.
Therefore, one should not deprive people of sleep.

Here, the conclusion does not strictly follow from the premises. But nor is there even an implicit moral premise, such as 'torture is wrong'. Because the premises are merely descriptive, the prescriptive conclusion does not follow.

The is/ought gap is, then, at least on one reading, an uncontroversial point about the logic of moral arguments. Unless at least one premise contains a prescriptive element, one can never reach a prescriptive conclusion.

Prescriptivism accepts the is/ought gap and understands moral judgements to have a special prescriptive character which makes them fundamentally different from merely descriptive statements.

Such a view seems to run into a problem, however. If moral judgements are not descriptive, and therefore neither true nor false, how does one reason about them? This echoes the problem which faced emotivism. If ethics is just about preferences or feelings, what has reason got to do with it?

The distinctive feature of prescriptivism is its claim that this problem only appears to arise because we hold the false view that it is only possible to reason about descriptive claims. Prescriptivists show how this view is wrong simply by providing examples of how it is possible to reason about things that are not factual and analysing the rules which govern such forms of reasoning. For instance, 'Go to London now!' is neither true nor false, but that doesn't mean I can't reason about it. First, if someone utters inconsistent imperatives, it is reason that picks up on that inconsistency. It is clear that 'Stay here!' is inconsistent with 'Go to London now!' and spotting this inconsistency means applying rules of reasoning. So one way in which reasoning is important in ethics is that it is important for consistency.

Another role for reason is connected with the idea that any ethical principle must be universalisable. Universalisability has been acknowledged by many moral theorists as a key feature of ethical judgements. What it means is that to say something is right or wrong is to make a general claim that it is always right or wrong in relevantly similar circumstances. For example, if I say that it is wrong for you to torment your hamster, part of what it means to say it is wrong is that it would also be wrong for other people to torment other hamsters in similar situations. This is an instance of how any particular moral judgement – *that* is wrong – can be universalised to a related universal moral judgement – *all such acts* are wrong.

The importance of universalisability for ethics is apparent in the way in which we call people who do not universalise moral judgements hypocrites. For instance, a person who claims adultery is wrong but who commits adultery himself is called a hypocrite. This only makes sense if we assume that by saying 'adultery is wrong', they mean that rule to cover all cases of adultery. Hence, the idea that moral principles are in this sense universal seems integral to the very idea of a moral principle.

Universalisability does not imply crude generalising. A situation may include very specific features, such that no-one else would ever be in the same position, in which case no general rule can be inferred from it. But none the less, it is part of what it means to act wrongly in that case that anyone else in the same situation would be wrong to do the same.

As the examples of consistency and universalisability show, it does seem to be the case that there is plenty of room for reason to have a role in ethics, even if ethics is non-descriptive and hence non-factual. However, there are criticisms that could be laid at prescriptivism's door.

First, there is the problem of its internalism. Internalism claims that to say 'I ought to do X' is to commit oneself to doing X. But if that were true, surely it would be self-contradictory to say 'I ought to, but I don't'. Yet we say things like this all the time and we don't seem to be contradicting ourselves when we do.

Hare replies to this criticism by pointing out that the 'but' proves there is something wrong with saying this kind of thing. To say 'I ought to, but don't' is to acknowledge an inconsistency, which is to admit either that one doesn't sincerely think one ought to do the thing, or that there is some other reason holding you back, such as weakness of will (*akrasia*).

A second difficulty is that although prescriptivism gives reason a role in ethics, it is not clear that this role is sufficiently wide-ranging. For instance, what if I say everyone able to afford it ought to sacrifice a banana to the God of breakfast every Sunday morning? This principle does seem to be universalisable and it need not be inconsistent with any other moral beliefs. In that sense, it satisfies the rational constraints prescriptivism demands. But surely such a moral judgement is absurd and it must be possible to criticise its rationality. However, it is not clear that prescriptivism can tell us how rationality can be invoked to criticise this moral principle.

We have spent some time looking at prescriptivism as an attempt to develop a sophisticated non-cognitivist ethics. We have here, of course, merely scratched the surface of the debate. But we need to move on because the cognitivist/ non-cognitivist distinction is not the only important one in meta-ethics. Perhaps even more important is the distinction between deontological, consequentialist and virtue ethics.

▶ Deontological and consequentialist ethics

Travelling in a hostile land divided by bitter civil war with 20 other innocent civilians, you are stopped by some local militia. They accuse you and your friends of being spies for the enemy. They threaten to execute all of you unless you prove that you are on their side by shooting a civilian they have captured from the enemy side, whose only crime is to be from a different ethnic group to that of the militia. Your choice is stark: take one innocent life yourself or allow someone else to take 21. What do you do?

There are at least two ways to think about this horrible moral dilemma. One is to say that you should do whatever has the best net consequences. Since one course of action will lead to the loss of 21 innocent lives and the other only one, and since there is no third option available, the morally right thing to do is to kill the innocent prisoner yourself. An ethic which reasons in this way is known as consequentialist, since it looks at the consequences of an action when judging its moral value.

A second way of thinking about this is that you have two choices of action. One choice involves you killing and the other does not. Killing is morally wrong, not killing is morally acceptable. Therefore, there is only one morally wrong choice you can make here, and that is to kill the innocent prisoner. So the moral thing to do is to refuse and face the consequences. An ethic which reasons in this way is known as deontological (from the Greek word *deon*, meaning duty).

The difference between the two approaches is stark in this particular example. In general, the difference is that the deontologist claims that certain acts are wrong in themselves, no matter what the consequence are. The consequentialist, on the other hand, claims that no acts are right or wrong in themselves, but only in virtue of the consequences they produce. So even cannibalism could be morally acceptable, if the consequences of it are good, as they might be when the survivors of a disaster can only stay alive long enough to escape or be rescued by eating human flesh.

The difference between the two views is perhaps best captured by looking at the different ways each one relates the rightness or wrongness of actions to the goodness or badness of situations. Consequentialism defines what is right in terms of the good. In other words, the right thing to do just is what produces the better outcome. For the deontologist, what is right and what is good are distinct. It may be right to do something which doesn't produce the best outcome, such as refusing to shoot the innocent prisoner even though more people die as a result of your decision than otherwise would have done. In the same way, it might be wrong to do something which does produce the best outcome, such as going ahead and executing the prisoner.

The distinction can also be understood in terms of means and ends. For the consequentialist, the good should be obtained by all means necessary. For the deontologist, the ends do not justify the means. It is what is done rather than the consequences of what is done which are all important.

Both views have their critics. Consequentialism is often criticised for not respecting the autonomy of persons, which is the view that people should be free to pursue their own interests, just so long as they do not harm others. For the consequentialist, it is possible to deny a person this right if it means that more good consequences would result. For example, it might be okay to kill the innocent prisoner or otherwise harm innocent people in order to produce the best overall outcome. In this way, consequentialism contradicts the great deontological philosopher, Immanuel Kant, who argued that people should always be treated as ends in themselves, and never as mere means to an end.

This criticism can, however, be turned back on to the deontologist. Could we not argue that in the innocent prisoner example, to refuse to kill one person and so allow 21 to die is to use the lives of those 20 other people as a means of keeping oneself morally pure? How can we be valuing their lives as ends in themselves if we are prepared to allow them all to be killed so that we can avoid personally doing wrong?

Consequentialists criticise deontologists for failing to consider impartially the interests of persons. This is the requirement some see as central to ethics to consider all people equally, and to give no special weight to myself or others close to me. In deciding to take one life to save 21 we respect this view because we are considering everyone's interests and acting in the interests of as many people as possible. The deontologist, it is claimed, does not consider impartially the interests of all persons, but merely seeks to avoid personal wrongdoing.

Deontological views are also criticised for being too narrow. For instance, one deontological principle is the principle of double effect. On this view, an act is only wrong if there is a bad intention as well as a bad action. So, for example, to cause death by shooting is not wrong unless the shot was intended to kill. This may seen reasonable, but the principle of double effect allows one to do something which one knows will do harm, as long as one does not intend that harm. So if, for example, I know that phoning someone will trigger a bomb to go off, but my intention is not to set off a bomb, merely to make a phone call, it seems that I do no wrong by making the call. This is an example of how deontology may be too narrow, in that it allows us to do many things, even things with bad consequences, just as long as we avoid directly doing wrong ourselves.

In response, consequentialism can be accused of having too wide a scope. Almost everything we do has consequences. For instance, if I buy a jacket which is made in a Third World sweat-shop, my action has bad consequences for workers in the Third World since it supports a bad form of production rather than a benign one. On the consequentialist view, because this action has a bad consequence, it is morally wrong. But if we follow the logic of this through, it seems we are constantly responsible for a whole myriad of wrongdoings. If I have a cup of tea instead of helping the poor, someone might die. Does that mean I did the wrong thing by having a drink?

This difference between the narrow and wide scope of deontological and consequentialist ethics is a key divider. It is perhaps best captured in the differing attitudes of both views to the acts–omissions distinction. Acts are things we do and omissions things we do not do. A classic example which highlights the distinction is the difference between allowing someone on a life-support machine to die by not giving them food or medicine (an omission) or helping them to die by switching off the machine (an act). The consequentialist sees both the act and the omission as morally equivalent, since their consequences are the same and we have the same degree of choice in both. For the deontologist, there is a clear difference: one is killing and one is letting die, and one could be wrong while the other be right.

In summary, deontological rules are weak and exclusory. They leave many areas of our lives untouched and tend to focus on what we shouldn't do, not what we should. Consequentialist rules are strong and inclusory. They affect all our decisions and determine how we should behave in a wide range of circumstances.

▶ Virtue ethics

For many years, ethics courses in British and American universities would discuss the deontological/consequentialist distinction as though it offered an either/or choice of meta-ethical framework. But in recent years, there has been an increasing interest in a third way. Virtue ethics, however, is not a new-fangled innovation but owes its origins to the moral philosophy of Aristotle.

Virtue ethics puts the character of the agent at the centre of morality. Rather than looking outside of the agent at what the right acts are or what the consequences of actions are, and then saying that the morally good person must do these acts, virtue ethics starts by looking at the morally good person and determines what is good on the basis of what such a person would do.

For example, consider the example of the innocent prisoner which we looked at above. Consequentialist and deontological approaches both offered very different solutions to the puzzle of what the right thing to do was. Both offered a pretty clear-cut solution. But this might strike us as very odd indeed. After all, what such hypothetical circumstances surely show more than anything is how agonising moral decisions can be. We should therefore be suspicious of any theory which offers a clear-cut, off-the-peg solution to such a dilemma.

How might virtue ethics offer a more plausible approach? First, it is unlikely that virtue ethics could provide any simple answer. Virtue ethics stresses that being good is a matter of character, and that character is something which is developed. It is about having certain dispositions and the wisdom to make good choices and judgements. It is not about being armed with a kind of moral calculus which allows you measure any act against an ethical scale and read off whether it is right or wrong. This stress on character and judgement over rules and principles means that virtue ethics rarely generates automatic responses to ethical dilemmas.

Nevertheless, if virtue ethics is to provide a plausible alternative to consequentialism or deontology, it must have something to say on this matter. If we are to consider how we should act in such a situation, we should consider how a virtuous person would act. To do this, one needs to build up a picture of the virtuous person. She will be thoughtful of others as well as herself. She will be averse to causing harm and will try and benefit as many people as possible. She will try not to reward wickedness or do wrong herself. She will respect other people.

In making this list you will notice that it includes virtues associated with both deontology and consequentialism. The desire to avoid harm and to benefit as many people as possible sounds very much like consequentialism. But to respect others and avoid wrongdoing sounds much more like deontology. This reflects the fact that both consequentialism and deontology are based on important moral considerations. Their alleged error is to focus too narrowly on just a few, instead of realising that a good person takes all into account and has to make a judgement in each case about what is the right thing to do.

Virtue ethics can sound very appealing but it does face several objections. In particular, it is very hard to see how it can actually tell us what to do. In this example, for instance, it is clear to see what the good person would be like and what kinds of considerations they would base their decision on. But can the theory actually tell us what to do, or whether the person who chooses one way or the other has done the right thing?

There is also a whiff of circularity about the idea of the virtuous person. The right thing to do is what the virtuous person would do. But what is the virtuous person if it is not the person who does the right thing? It seems that if we try and discover what the good person is, we end up saying it is the person who acts well; but when we try to find out what acting well is, we have to say it is acting how the virtuous person does. We never seem to get to the root of what makes things right.

Perhaps the issue will become clearer when we look at how these three meta-ethical frameworks – deontology, consequentialism and virtue ethics – are fleshed out in normative ethical theories. Remember that so far we have only been discussing the nature of morality. We have yet to consider what is actually right or wrong. When we do this, we can put flesh on the bones of our three meta-ethical theories and this will help us to assess their relative merits.

▶ Utilitarianism

Consequentialists say that one must do that which has the best consequences. But what are the best consequences? Utilitarians say that the morally right act is that which has the consequence of producing more 'utility' or usefulness. Only acts which benefit or harm somebody can be right or wrong.

The obvious next question is, in what way must our actions be useful for them to be good? In other words, what is utility? There are three main forms of utilitarianism, all of which answer this question differently. Classical or hedonic utilitarians say that utility is increasing the pleasure and reducing the pain of as many people as possible. Preference utilitarians say that utility is the satisfaction of the preferences of as many people as possible. Welfare utilitarians say that utility is improving the welfare of as many people as possible.

Classical utilitarianism is most closely associated with Jeremy Bentham (1748–1832) and John Stuart Mill (1806–1873). However, with its emphasis on pleasure or happiness as the highest good, many see it as taking too narrow a view of both what we want out of life and what we consider to be morally important. It is hard to see how acts of self-sacrifice, such as enduring torture to spare comrades, or giving our lives for others, can be described as the pursuit of pleasure. It is also clear, however, that these acts deserve our praise. The failings of this view are also made clear by the question, 'Would you rather be as you are, but unhappy, or reduced to the level of an imbecile and be happy for the rest of your life?' The mere fact that many would choose to be unhappy shows how we are not all the hedonists classical utilitarianism believe we are or should be.

Mill tried to answer this objection by distinguishing between the higher pleasures of the intellect and the lower pleasures of the body. The former are worth much more than the latter, so it is always preferable to at least be capable of enjoying such pleasure than being only capable of enjoying the simple pleasures of the flesh. The proof of this is that anyone who enjoyed both kinds of pleasure would always choose the higher over the lower. However, if what Mill really valued was pleasure and happiness, then how could he be so sure that a well-fed pig, for instance, does not enjoy more happiness than a miserable poet? If happiness really is the highest good, it is not obvious why so-called higher pleasures are superior, or that a person who was acquainted with both would necessarily chose them.

Preference utilitarianism aims to avoid the shortcomings of classical utilitarianism by saying we should attempt to satisfy our preferences. This has the advantage of allowing us more individual choice. Thus, if people prefer to live as happy imbeciles then so be it, but it would be wrong to enforce this option on those who would not prefer such a life or force those who do prefer it to change their lifestyle.

However, this view too has problems. First, some things are good whether people desire them or not. For example, it would be good to relieve the suffering of a minority, even if the majority don't want to. Second, some things are bad even if people do desire them. A Nazi government could be one such example. Critics say that preference utilitarianism reduces morality to the level of a free-market economy, where 'good' and 'bad' are simply defined in terms of what people want. Surely, it is argued, not all that is good is desired, and not all that is desired is good.

Welfare utilitarians claim that what is useful is what best fulfils the interests of people. This has to be distinguished from what people desire. People don't always desire what is in their best interests, hence the old saying 'be careful what you wish for, you might just get it'. There is also the problem that people's desires and preferences vary enormously, and thus it is very difficult to act according to people's desires. It is far easier to know what in general is good for people. This means welfare utilitarianism also has the advantage of being a practical doctrine. However, one major disadvantage of this theory is that it seems to be very paternalistic. We should do what is good for people whether they want it or not.

One problem faced by all these versions of utilitarianism is that perhaps there is no single good. We want to be happy, we want to make our own choices and we want our welfare to be considered by others. If we decide that just one of these things is the highest good, we inevitably miss some things out. But if we can't define utility clearly, then we can't come up with a clear account of what the right moral action is.

Another problem faced by all versions of utilitarianism is whether, when judging the utility of an action, each action should be taken on its own merits, or whether acts should be judged according to their general effect on utility. For example, although murder will generally reduce utility, there are bound to be some cases where it will not. In such a case, is it still not right to spare the life of the innocent victim? Some utilitarians would argue that it is. Because it is impossible to calculate the consequences of individual actions, it is better to follow general rules about what best serves utility. If we try to judge each case on its merits, we will make more mistakes than if we follow rules. So utility is best served by following rules rather than making decisions on a case by case basis. This view is known as rule, as opposed to act, utilitarianism.

The problem with rule utilitarianism is that there will always seem to be some occasion where the breaking of a generally held rule would be the right thing to do. Consider, for example, murdering someone who is about to kill someone else, stealing in order to stay alive or lying in order to save a life. In order to follow the spirit of utilitarianism, surely in these circumstances the rule should be abandoned and utility be maximised. The rule utilitarian could try and get around this by making her rules more specific. For example, the rule could be: 'Tell the truth unless lying saves lives'. But then in order to cover all possible eventualities, the rule would have to be: 'Tell the truth except when not telling the truth would promote greater utility'. But this would just be act utilitarianism all over again, as it would in effect mean, 'Tell the truth when that promotes utility and lie when that promotes utility', which means 'Do whatever promotes utility'.

Another problem for all versions of utilitarianism is that is seems that they all have the potential to conflict with rights. The maximising of utility – be it for preferences, welfare or pleasure – may be best served if a minority's rights are trampled over. Utility might also be best served if all people with damaged kidneys, for example, could be given transplants with kidneys taken from healthy people, without their consent. If all we are concerned about is the final outcome, why should we in principle be concerned about rights?

Many utilitarians accept this challenge. Bentham called natural rights 'nonsense on stilts' and argued that rights are merely useful constructs (see Chapter 5 on political philosophy). In any case, they argue that no utilitarian theory will, in practice, conflict with what we take to be basic rights, since a society where such 'rights' are ignored could not be one with high utility.

▶ Kantian ethics

The great German philosopher Immanuel Kant (1724–1804) developed the most famous version of deontological ethics. However, when one examines it one sees a very clear example of what I described earlier as the continuity between meta-ethics and normative ethics. Kant's ethics occupies a kind of half-way house between the two. It has more flesh on its bones than a mere meta-ethical theory but often seems to lack the firm guidance we might expect from a normative ethic.

Central to Kant's ethics is the idea of the categorical imperative. An imperative is a command, of the kind 'don't eat that second slice of cream cake' or 'do not lie'. Imperatives can be hypothetical (or conditional) or categorical. A hypothetical imperative is where the command contains an explicit or implicit 'if' clause. For example, the command 'Don't eat that second slice of cream cake' is hypothetical when it is followed by or assumes something like 'if you want to keep to your diet'. In such an instance, the command not to eat the cake is not absolute – the command should be followed only if you want to achieve some further aim or goal. If you do go ahead and eat the cake, you will have done the wrong thing only in regard to the goal of sticking to your diet.

Categorical imperatives, on the other hand, do not have any 'ifs'. When 'Do not lie' is uttered as a categorical imperative, the idea is that lying is something you should not do just because it is wrong, not because following the command is merely a means to achieve an end.

It should be clear that only categorical imperatives belong to morality. If you eat the second piece of cream cake, you have not been a bad person, you've just failed to achieve a goal. Only when you act against a categorical imperative do you behave immorally.

The hallmark of a categorical imperative is its universalisability (see the section on prescriptivism above). That is to say, an imperative can only be categorical if one could will that everyone followed the command. For example, 'Always tell the truth' and 'Lie to get what you want' both look as though they could be categorical imperatives. But whereas it is possible to will that everyone told the truth, one cannot will that everyone lied to get what they wanted. This is not because it is physically or psychologically impossible to will such a thing. Rather, it is that if everyone followed the command, its purpose would be undermined. In a society where everyone lies to get what they want, trust is impossible. This means that lying is no longer effective. You can only lie to get what you want if people generally accept what people say as the truth. So if everyone lies to try and get what they want, the power of the lie to achieve this goes. Thus, it would be in some sense irrational to will that everyone followed such a rule.

So, for Kant, moral rules are universalisable categorical imperatives. But the real question is, where do we get these categorical imperatives from? Kant's answer is hard to fathom. It has at its root the idea that each of us is a rational agent and that each of us is able to will – to desire or choose – freely and autonomously. Moral rules are derived when we use our rationality to guide our wills. It works something like this.

First, we recognise that what we will can be in the form of a categorical or hypothetical imperative. We can will things for some end or purpose (hypothetically) or will them for their own sake (categorically). Only the latter are moral commands. Such commands are, as we have seen, universalisable. Kant's idea is that when we reflect on this, we will see that there are a number of rules which we should follow because it is rational to follow them and they are categorical and universalisable in nature.

The example of telling a lie may help to illustrate this. It is clear that the rule 'do not lie' is categorical in nature. It is universalisable since we could, and perhaps should, will that no-one ever lied. Kant's idea is that on reflection we will see that it is rational to follow this rule. Reason, detached from any self-interest, just has to recognise that as a universalisable categorical imperative, it is a rule it makes sense to follow. Importantly for Kant, our decision to follow it is based not on emotion or character, but merely the will's decision to follow the dictates of reason.

The centrality of the autonomous will in Kant's ethics is illustrated by another general rule which Kant takes to follow from his principles. This is the idea that one should always treat persons as ends and never as mere means to an end. This is, on the one hand, merely the logical consequence of the categorical imperative: we can consistently desire that people be treated always as beings with value in themselves, but not that we treat them as mere means to an end. But perhaps it is also indicative of the supreme importance Kant places on the idea that we are individual moral agents with the freedom to choose.

The main problem with Kant's ethics is that it seems one can understand and accept it and still not know what one should do. Kant himself came up with several prescriptions, the injunction never to tell a lie being one. But it seems that one could will any number of moral rules to be followed with consistency. The idea that reason is somehow able to determine which of these rules we should follow and which we should not seems rather optimistic.

Hume famously said that 'reason is the slave of the passions', by which he meant reason alone can never provide us with a motivation to act, it can only help guide us to achieve what we desire. This directly contradicts Kant's view that reason can provide us with motives to act. If Hume is right, Kant's ethics is doomed.

It is true of this whole book that the issues discussed have depths we can merely skim the surface of. But this is particularly true of Kant. His arguments on this topic are difficult and require a close and detailed study to really comprehend and assess. This means that they can appear weaker in précis than alternatives which, on closer examination, are no stronger at all.

▶ Aristotelian ethics

Aristotle (384–322 BCE) was the father of virtue ethics. When it came to putting flesh on these moral bones and providing us with an actual guide to life, Aristotle's key idea was that of the golden mean.

In mathematics, the mean is the average of a series of two or more numbers. So, for example, the mean of two and six is four. Aristotle borrows this idea and applies it to the virtues, although it should be stressed that Aristotle's mean is not something that can be calculated with mathematical precision.

In ethics, the mean is the ideal point which lies between two extremes. For example, many consider courage to be a virtue. Typically, we think of courage to be a virtue with a vice – cowardice – which is its opposite. But on Aristotle's view, courage is actually the ideal that lies between two extremes – cowardice at one end and rashness at the other. Rashness is a kind of excess of courage, while cowardice is a deficiency of it.

The same model applies to all the other virtues. Honesty is a virtue of which dishonesty is a deficiency and something like tactlessness is the excess. Helpfulness is a virtue of which unhelpfulness is the deficiency and servility the excess. Modesty is a virtue of which reticence is the excess and boastfulness the deficiency.

The mean provides a principle which helps us to modify our characters in order to achieve what Aristotle called *Eudaimonia*, which means happiness or flourishing. The problem is that the doctrine of the mean does not prescribe exactly what the ideal between the two extremes is, it just tells us virtue is to be found there. This is consistent with Aristotle's view that ethics is not a precise science and judgement is required to get things right. The doctrine of the mean points us in the right direction, but it doesn't give us a simple list of things we have to do in order to live well. (For more on Aristotle's ethics, see the companion volume to this book, *Philosophy: Key Texts*.)

▶ Animal rights

So far we have looked at issues in meta-ethics and normative ethics. Finally, we can turn to where the real 'action' is – applied ethics. What people most want to know about in ethics is what we should actually do. Applied ethics is about considering real ethical dilemmas and applying ethical principles to them. Here, we will look at three issues and consider just a few ways in which we can argue about them.

The issue of animal rights is one hotly contested area in ethics. While millions of people routinely eat factory-farmed animals, many others refuse to do so, seeing it as barbaric and cruel. Back in the nineteenth century, Jeremy Bentham made the case for treating animals better when he said, 'The question is not, Can they *reason*? nor Can they *talk*? but, Can they *suffer*?' The fact that animals do suffer has been at the basis of many arguments for animal rights ever since.

However, before going on, it should be pointed out that the phrase 'animal rights' may not be helpful. People who object to eating meat, for instance, may do so, not because they feel animals have rights, but just because they think there is something wrong about causing them to suffer. The idea of a 'right' is very specific and one should refrain from using the word unless one is talking about rights specifically.

Returning to the issue at hand, a typical argument for the better treatment of animals runs something like this:

Animals feel pain.
No innocent being should have pain inflicted on it unnecessarily.
Therefore, animals should not have pain inflicted on them unnecessarily.

This argument is valid in that, if the first two premises are true, the conclusion necessarily follows. In assessing the argument, we therefore need to consider whether the premises are true and, if they are, what follows from the conclusion.

As regards the first premise, one may ask, 'How do we know that animals feel pain?' The problem with this question is that it seems we can never know for sure that *any* living creature feels pain, including other human beings. However, by observing the behaviour of animals, and noting the basic similarities between the nervous systems of animals and humans, we can be much more sure that they do feel pain than that they don't. To demand more certainty than this would seem to be inappropriate, as we don't demand this certainty with fellow humans. Hence, the first premise does seem to be secure.

The second premise is deliberately worded with care. It contains the word 'innocent' because it would not be wrong to cause, for example, an attacker pain if that were our only means of defence. It contains the word 'unnecessary' because sometimes pain is required for a greater good. A dentist does not do something morally wrong when she hurts us administering an injection of anaesthetic.

This premise has an intuitive appeal. Surely, if we could choose between a world with a certain amount of pain and a world with twice this amount of pain, with no further benefit to the world with more pain, we would choose the first world. Unnecessary pain is unequivocally bad, and to ask why is to ask an inappropriate question. If we accept this, then not to count animal pain would seem arbitrary and unfair. The philosopher Richard Ryder calls this disregard of animals purely because they are not human 'speciesism'. Just as it is wrong not to take account of people's interests purely because of their race, sex or skin colour, so it would be wrong not to take account of an animal's interests purely on the grounds of species.

Against the second premise, it could be argued that pain itself is neither good nor bad and it is thus neither right nor wrong to cause it. This may seem implausible, but one could distinguish between pain and suffering. Only animals with highly developed consciousness can truly suffer, it is argued. Without this, the feeling of pain is merely transitory, a reflex response by the body. It is nonsense to talk of pain being bad for a goldfish. The goldfish merely feels the pain and then forgets about it. With humans, though, we dread and remember pain, and this is what makes it so intolerable in excess.

Against this objection, two points could be raised. First, surely some animals do suffer as well as feel pain. Given the difficulty of drawing a line between these two so-called different states, it is better to err on the side of caution, and not cause pain to any animal. Second, even if the distinction is a good one, it is still hard to see how this makes the causing of 'mere' pain a matter of indifference.

A further objection to the premise is that the idea of unnecessary pain makes it too vague. Given that all pains are not equal (compare a pinprick with severe nausea), isn't a bit of animal pain a small price to pay for the pleasure and nutrients given to humans? Animal pain that we cause is not unnecessary: it serves our interests.

But in modern societies, it is hard to see how the causing of pain in hunting and farming is necessary. We don't need meat to live. In fact, some surveys suggest vegetarians live longer than their carnivorous contemporaries. So it's hard to see how such pain is necessary, on any definition of the word.

What if we accepted this argument as valid and sound? Well, it would be enough to show that we should grant animals something like rights, because it argues for the moral need to take into account the interests of animals. But how far would these rights extend? In the case of vivisection (animal testing) for cosmetics, which causes much pain and is clearly unnecessary (we have enough safe cosmetic ingredients for even the most demanding of faces), this would be deemed morally unacceptable. In the case of vivisection for medical purposes, we would have to balance out the benefits gained by eliminating the suffering of sick humans against the suffering inflicted on the animals experimented on. This is very difficult, because we would have to compare the pain and suffering of many different species.

In a surprising way, the argument above may actually support humane farming. Though factory-farmed animals certainly suffer unnecessary pain, humanely reared animals probably live a life more pain free than they would in the wild. And if death came easily, there would seem to be no objection, with this argument, to eating meat. Hunting is a different matter, however, although pro-hunting campaigners claim that hunting is necessary to control the fox population.

▶ Abortion

Perhaps the best way to approach this issue is to consider two arguments against abortion, as set out (and subsequently criticised) by Peter Singer in *Practical Ethics* (1979). All we can do here is just sketch out the key debating points in the argument. There are two versions, one of which considers innocent human beings, the other of which considers potential human beings:

> It is wrong to kill an innocent/potential human being.
> A human foetus is an innocent/potential human being.
> Therefore, it is wrong to kill a human foetus.

This argument alone throws up enough questions to ensure a lifetime of debate. Perhaps its most contentious point is the second premise. Is it true that a foetus is a human being?

The question of when a foetus becomes a human being is a difficult one. What is clear is that the development of the foetus is gradual and there is no 'magic moment' when it becomes a full human being. However, perhaps this should not concern us as much as it often does. After all, there is no 'magic moment' on the colour spectrum when yellow becomes green, but yellow and green are still different. In the same way, the fact that there is no clear boundary between foetus and fully developed human does not mean there is no distinction at all.

Even so, many problems remain. Some argue that the foetus is not a life in its own right, it is just a part of the mother. The plausibility of this depends very much on what stage of the pregnancy one is talking about. When the foetus is viable (able to survive outside the womb), it no longer seems plausible to say that the foetus is just a part of the mother.

Another issue regards the question of whether the significant factor is species membership or personhood. The foetus could be considered as a member of the species *homo sapiens* from an early age. But is this what makes its life valuable? Many believe that what we really value about human life is the fact that we are persons: independent, thinking, feeling beings with a sense of self. This is what makes it wrong to kill a human, not the fact that it belongs to a certain species. If we met a pig that had these human capabilities, it would be as wrong to kill it as it would be to kill a human. On this argument, the crucial point is not whether the foetus is a human, but whether it is a person, and until it has reached a certain level of development, it cannot be said to be a person in this sense.

So a central issue here is the actual status of the foetus. The argument against abortion set out above can be challenged if we question the status granted to the foetus in the second premise.

The first premise can also be attacked. Is it always wrong to kill a human being? On one version of the argument, it is stated that it is wrong to kill a potential human being. However, we don't in general grant the same rights to a potential something as to an actual something. In the USA, everyone is a potential president, but only the actual president has the rights and privileges of his office. So if the foetus is only a potential human or person, rather than an actual one, we may not agree that it is necessarily wrong to kill it. The value of a potential life cannot be assumed to be the same as that of an actual life.

More generally, we might ask whether the value of a life depends upon how well developed a being's capacities for thought, pain, pleasure and so on are. Even if we grant that a foetus is a human being; until it can feel or think, is it really as wrong to kill it as it is to kill a thinking, feeling creature? As Peter Singer controversially puts it, why do some people think it is so terrible to kill what is little more than a cluster of developing cells when they think it merely regrettable to kill an unwanted adult dog, which has feelings and possibly even thoughts?

▶ Euthanasia

Euthanasia is another controversial topic in ethics. Euthanasia is the providing of an easy and painless death. It can be voluntary, involuntary or non-voluntary. Involuntary euthanasia is killing against the wishes of the person being killed. It is straightforwardly murder and is not a form of euthanasia that is widely discussed in applied ethics. Non-voluntary euthanasia is killing where the person being killed is unable to give consent. For example, if someone is in an irreversible coma, we might think it right to end their life. But we cannot ask them permission to do so.

Perhaps the most pressing issues surround voluntary euthanasia. This is where people, often suffering with a painful, terminal illness, want the help of doctors to end their life before it becomes intolerable. This is often called assisted suicide, because these are cases where the person involved would commit suicide if they had the means to do so painlessly. But usually the help of doctors is required to ensure painless and easy death, so suicide is not an option.

Here, one way to argue is to start from the assumption that we have the right to make major life decisions for ourselves and seek to place the burden of proof on those who say this doesn't apply in euthanasia. Set out formally, the argument would look something like this:

Human beings have the right to make major life decisions for themselves.
The decision to end one's life is a major life decision.
Therefore, human beings have the right to make the decision to end their own lives.

One might think this argument is inadequate because euthanasia requires the help of another person. But while it does not establish the right to demand that someone help you end your life, it does seem enough to establish your right to ask and be helped if someone chooses to help. In general, if one has a right to do something, one also has a right to be helped voluntarily to do that if one cannot achieve it oneself.

How might someone attack this argument? The best route in would be to question the first premise. Maybe we don't have the right to make decisions about all major life choices and life and death is one such exception to this rule. It might be argued that life is sacred, and that it is always wrong to take it. Therefore, it is as wrong to take one's own life as it is to take the life of another and so this is one area of life where we do not have the right to choose for ourselves.

However, we do not generally think life is sacred in this way. Soldiers will shoot colleagues on the battlefield, for example, if they see that they are in pain and have no hope of being saved. We put down animals that are suffering rather than see them continue to suffer. Anyone who approves of abortion or meat eating also thinks that certain types of life are not sacred. The key question here, then, is, when must life be preserved and when is it acceptable or preferable to end it?

▶ Approaches to applied ethics

These short discussions are just examples of how we might approach moral issues. There are a few general features about them worth noting. First, applied ethics is sometimes described as applying normative theories to actual issues. This is certainly one way of going about it and we could have simply tried to apply utilitarianism, Kantian or Aristotelian ethics to the issues of animal welfare, abortion and euthanasia. For example, applying utilitarianism to abortion, we could ask: Is the general happiness best served by abortion? Should happiness be maximised or should only the happiness of already existing people be maximised? If the bringing of new life increases happiness, then can we not produce the same or a greater amount of happiness by having an abortion and having another child at a different, more suitable time? This is certainly one approach and I would encourage the reader to think about how one might apply the normative theories we have looked at to specific issues. But what the short discussions of the three topics have made clear, I hope, is that there can be much fruitful discussion in applied ethics which is not about simply applying a normative theory. Often, we can make great progress just by setting out the basic objections or arguments in support of ethical stances and closely examining them. This is very important, for if applied ethics were just about applying normative theories, agreement among people who disagree about normative theories would be much harder to achieve.

A second general point is that discussions in applied ethics often confuse what is legal and what is moral. The two realms are distinct, though hopefully related. Applied ethics is about deciding what is right or wrong. We may decide that something is right which is currently illegal, or something is wrong which is currently legal.

▶ Conclusion

Moral philosophy is an exciting field of philosophy. It is where the real-life application of philosophy is most apparent. But at the same time, to do it properly one needs to spend a lot of time considering issues of meta-ethics which take one far from the concerns of everyday moral choices. What one needs to remember is that the concerns of meta-ethics, normative ethics and applied ethics are not absolutely distinct. The boundaries between these three parts of the subject are fluid. But at the same time, it is not always necessary to call upon the resources of all three. One does not need to have a complete meta-ethical and normative framework in place before one can address issues of practical ethics. Sometimes good arguments and sound reasoning are enough.

Summary

Ethics is concerned with the issue of how we ought to live, not in order to achieve a particular goal, but in order to live a good life in general.

At the most abstract level, meta-ethics is about the general nature of morality. Moral realists believe that moral judgements express truths which exist independently of humanity. Cognitivists add that these truths can be known. Non-realists believe that moral judgements do not have this objective existence. It follows that they are non-cognitivists, as these moral truths cannot be known since they do not exist. A simple non-cognitivist position, such as emotivism, holds that moral judgements are no more than an expression of an opinion or a taste. More sophisticated non-cognitivist positions, such as prescriptivism, hold that although moral judgements are neither true nor false, it is none the less possible to reason about them and disagree about matters of ethics on rational grounds.

Ethical theories can be deontological, consequentialist or virtue-based. Deontologists hold that acts are right or wrong depending on the nature of the act itself, not because of its consequences. Consequentialists argue, to the contrary, that things are only wrong if they cause harm and right if they make things better. Proponents of virtue ethics argue that morality has its basis in the character of the moral agent, not in an analysis of the right or wrong of particular actions.

When we move from the general nature of morality to actual moral codes, we move to the arena of normative ethics. Utilitarianism is a normative consequentialist ethic. It holds that acts are right if they increase utility and wrong if they decrease it. Utility can be understood as happiness, the ability to select either for what one prefers or for one's welfare.

Kantian ethics is a deontological ethic. It holds that we should only follow moral rules which we can consistently will to hold as universal rules. To act morally we have to act out of a pure will to follow morality and not out of any other motive or just habit.

Aristotelian ethics is a virtue ethic. It holds that the good person develops virtues which lie at a mid-point or 'mean' between two extremes. For example, generosity is the mean between meanness and profligacy.

When we discuss particular issues in ethics, we move from normative to applied ethics. One normative question is how we should treat animals and whether their capacity to feel pain grants them rights. Another is the issue of abortion, and whether it is ever right to kill a foetus. A third is the issue of euthanasia and whether it is permissible to help someone take their own life.

Glossary

Acts–omissions The distinction between things we do which bring about a certain consequence and things we do not do, with the same consequence.

Akrasia Weakness of will, when we do something we know to be wrong.

Applied ethics The area of ethics concerned with the rights and wrongs of particular issues.

Good   Good and bad describe states of affairs or persons, in contrast to right and wrong which describe the morality of actions.

Internalism   The theory that if one believes something to be wrong, one is necessarily motivated not to do it.

Is/ought gap   The impossibility of deducing matters of value from matters of fact. Also known as the fact–value distinction.

Meta-ethics   The area of ethics concerned with the general nature of morality.

Non-cognitivism   The view that moral truths cannot be known, because there are no moral truths independent of persons.

Normative ethics   The area of ethics concerned with particular theories of right and wrong.

Relativism   The idea that there are no universal moral truths and that right and wrong are always relative to a society, group or individual.

Universalisability   The feature of moral judgements that they apply to everyone at all times equally.

Further reading

In the companion volume to his book, *Philosophy: Key Texts*, I look at two books which focus on ethics: Aristotle's *Nichomachean Ethics*, which is the classic text of virtue ethics, and Sartre's *Existentialism and Humanism*. Both are very accessible, interesting works.

Other classic texts worth reading include Hume's *An Enquiry concerning the Principles of Morals*, which is a brilliant early non-cognitivist work; Kant's *Groundwork of the Metaphysics of Morals*, a difficult but rewarding exposition of a deontological ethic; and Mills's *Utilitarianism*, the classic exposition of the eponymous theory.

Some accessible twentieth-century texts include *Writings on an Ethical Life* by the utilitarian Peter Singer (Fourth Estate); *Moral Luck* by Bernard Williams (Cambridge University Press); and, for a more demanding read, *Reasons and Persons* by Derek Parfit (Oxford University Press).

A Companion to Ethics, edited by Peter Singer (Blackwell), is a superb collection of short essays on a broad range of ethical issues. *Being Good* by Simon Blackburn (Oxford University Press) is one of the best short introductions to ethics.

3 Philosophy of Mind

▶ What is the philosophy of mind?

The universe contains many amazing things. At the smallest level there are inconceivably small particles with exotic names such as quarks and neutrinos. These form the basic building blocks of atoms such as hydrogen and nitrogen. From these atoms the whole material world is formed, from tiny organisms such as amoeba, to large mammals such as elephants. There are mountains, oceans and forests of infinite variety.

The earth itself is only one planet in one solar system. Our sun is inconceivably hot, planets such as Jupiter inconceivably large. And our solar system is itself just one small corner of the universe, an unfathomably vast, expanding cradle of space and time.

We understand more about the universe than ever before. We understand it thanks to the growth of knowledge in the physical sciences. All I have described so far is explained within the terms of science, with reference to the behaviour of physical matter. But one thing does not seem to be included in this picture. Perhaps ironically, perhaps tellingly, the one thing physical science does not seem to be able to explain is what makes its own explanations possible: the existence of minds. It is our minds which have enabled us to understand the universe as much as we do, yet this understanding has not extended to the subject of that understanding: human consciousness.

The problem of how the existence of minds fits into our understanding of the world is central to the philosophy of mind. In particular, it has led to one key question which is still unresolved: the so-called mind–body problem. This is the problem of how the mental is related to the physical, and in particular, how our minds, our thoughts, our feelings and sensations are related to our bodies, matter, atoms and so on. Although there are other problems in the philosophy of mind, such as the problem of other minds, the possibility of unconscious mental states and personal identity, the mind–body problem is by far and away the dominant issue in the field. For that reason, we will first look at various solutions to the mind–body problem: dualism, behaviourism, physicalism and functionalism.

But before we begin, a word of caution. Most solutions to the mind–body problem offer an answer to the question of what mind is, which is supposed to make its relationship to body explicable. So we get a statement, 'Mind is X'. The problem is that not all statements of the form 'X is Y' are identity statements, and not all identity statements appear to mean precisely the same thing.

For example, consider these statements, which are all of the form X is Y:

1　Gary Parry is the Prime Minister of Ruritania.
2　Money is the root of all evil.
3　A noun is a word which labels a thing or an idea.
4　Dough is flour, yeast and water.
5　A cat is a feline.
6　Bill Stickers is innocent.
7　Water is H_2O.

We can discern several different usages of 'is' here. One is the 'is' of identity. In such sentences, 'is' can be replaced by 'is the same as' without any loss of meaning. There is also the 'is' of definition. In addition, there is the 'is' of predication is where 'is' introduces a description of some kind. One may be able to discern other ways of describing the function of the verb 'to be' in these sentences. I will leave it to the reader to ponder which usage of 'is' occurs in each sentence. I expect you will find that it is less obvious which is the best way to describe each use of 'is' than you would at first think it is.

We will be considering as we go along the significance of the different ways in which 'mind is X' can be understood as we go along. At this stage, it is important simply to note that there is an ambiguity in saying 'mind is X'. The problem we will see is that when different theorists claim mind is such and such and others disagree, they're not always using 'is' in the same way.

▶ Dualism

One theory of mind with a long history is dualism. Dualism comes in various forms, and we will be considering the most prominent, substance dualism (hereafter, simply dualism). Substance dualism is the view that mind and matter are two different kinds of 'stuff'. Matter is what the physical sciences deal with and is the stuff out of which all the things in the universe mentioned at the start of this chapter are made. Mind, however, is a different kind of substance which is not the subject of physical science, but which none the less exists within conscious beings such as ourselves.

To see why some people believe dualism is true, it is necessary to consider the metaphysics of identity. The classic principles of identity are, first, Leibniz's Law, after the philosopher who wrote it, and, second, the principle of the identity of indiscernibles. They say:

1 *Leibniz's Law.* If A is identical to B, then any property of A is a property of B, or whatever is true of A is true of B.
2 *The principle of the identity of indiscernibles.* If A and B are identical in all respects, then they are identical objects, i.e. one and the same object.

If identity is understood in these ways – and philosophers generally agree that identity should be understood along these lines – then if one thing is identical with another, both must occupy the same time and space and have identical properties. This seems to be true. If John is blind and Smith can see, Smith can't be John. Nor can Smith be John if Smith is now in Lanzarote and John is in Huddersfield. But if all that is true of John is true of Smith, they must be the same person.

One must be careful to note here that the properties which identical objects share must include spacio–temporal location – where they are in time and space. If two things are in different places but have all other properties the same, they are only *qualitatively* identical, not *quantitatively* or *numerically* identical. So, two billiard balls off the same production line are only qualitatively identical. Julian Baggini and the author of this book, however, are quantitatively identical. It is the latter form of identity which is the subject of Leibniz's Law and which concerns us here.

The simplest argument for dualism is based simply on these principles of identity. The argument starts by looking at the properties of mind and matter, which includes our physical bodies.

When we consider the properties of matter, we could count among them the fact that matter exists in definite moments of time and space. You can always say where and when a bit of matter is, to the nanometre, if you have precise enough equipment. (This may not be true of the very smallest level – the level of quantum physics – but since quantum theory is very much cutting-edge science and not yet properly understood even by specialists in the field, we should not be too hasty in jumping to conclusions on the basis of its findings so far.) Another feature of matter is that it is in principle observable by all. With a powerful enough microscope, one could see even the smallest particles. Finally, matter is subject to the laws of physics and, except at the level of its most elementary particles, is always divisible.

When you turn now to mind, you find that it doesn't seem to fit the same description. A thought cannot be located in space and time in the same way as a particle or object can. It just doesn't seem to make sense to say that a thought occurred three inches behind my nose, for example. Nor are minds in principle observable by anyone. You cannot 'look into my mind' in anything other than a figurative sense. Thoughts, feelings and sensations do not seem to be suitable subjects for the laws of physics – it is not gravity that brings our thoughts down to earth. Mind also seems to be essentially indivisible. My consciousness cannot be split up into infinitely small parts – it forms a whole.

Mind also seems to have a special feature for us which matter doesn't. I can be in error about features of the external world. But I cannot be in error about the state of my own mind. If I think I can see a yellow canary, I could be mistaken that there is a canary, but not that I am having a visual experience that seems to be of a canary.

We can set out these differences between the properties of mind and matter and see how they starkly contrast with one another.

Mind	Body/Matter
Exists in time, but not in space	Exists in space and time
Private, i.e. is only directly observable by the person who has the mind	Is directly observable by all.
Is not subject to laws of physics	Is subject to laws of physics
We cannot be in error about states of our minds	We can be in error about states of the physical world
Cannot be divided	Can be divided

If this is a genuine set of differences, we can easily apply Leibniz's Law to produce the following argument:

1 If mind is identical to matter, then mind must have all the same properties as matter.
2 Mind has different properties to matter (see table).
3 Therefore, mind is not identical to matter.

What then is mind? Given that matter is a kind of substance, it seems natural to suppose that mind must be some other kind of substance. Hence, we reach the conclusion of dualism: that there are two types of substance in the world: mind and matter. Dualism is a view that has dominated the thinking of mankind for centuries, and is central to most religious conceptions of persons. Such is its acceptance that Gilbert Ryle, writing after the Second World War, dubbed it 'the Official Doctrine'.

The merits of dualism are that it fits in with our intuitive views about the mind, and the argument for it is straightforward. It has proved to be a very resilient view, and despite the rise of physicalism and scientism, many, if not most, people still subscribe to it. But it is also perhaps the most criticised view in the philosophy of mind.

▶ Arguments against dualism

One major difficulty with dualism is the problem of interaction. We have an idea of how matter affects matter. As they are fundamentally the same kind of substance, any two bits of matter can interact with one another. But how can mind interact with matter if they are fundamentally different types of thing? If mind is not in space, how can it affect or be affected by things in space? How can a thing without mass move a thing with mass?

Mind and body clearly do interact, and that interaction is at least sometimes causal in nature. My decisions seem to be able to cause my arm to move. Physical objects can make me think, or give me perceptions. But the only way we can understand causation is on the principle that like affects like. If mind is not at all like matter, the possibility of interaction seems to disappear.

One reply would be that if the argument for dualism is good and interaction is a fact, it must be true that mind and matter can interact. Just because we can't understand how they interact doesn't mean dualism is wrong. We should not use our lack of understanding to criticise dualism. What is more, why should we assume that all forms of interaction must fit the model of physical causation? Isn't that just a bias we have in favour of our most successful theories? Just because the physical sciences have explained a lot, it doesn't mean they explain everything. You could even argue that we have not explained physical causation at all. All we have done is found the laws that govern causation. But we don't know why things should cause other things to happen at all.

The interaction problem identifies a puzzle in dualism; it does not attack the argument for it. Other criticisms are directed at the argument itself. A popular one is based on a logical mistake called the masked man fallacy. Here's an example of the fallacy at work. I know who John is, but at a party I see a masked man, and I don't know who he is. Under Leibniz's Law, if John is identical to the masked man then everything which is true of John must be true of the masked man. But it is true of the masked man that I don't know who he is and it is true of John that I do know who he is. So John can't be the masked man.

This is clearly absurd. There is nothing in this situation which rules out John being the masked man. So is Leibniz's Law wrong? Not at all. The fallacy hinges on the fact that I may know X under one description, but not under another description. Facts like these are irrelevant to what is really true of the thing itself. What I know about John and the masked man are thus not real properties of either of them. They say something about me, not them.

What this teaches us is that what we believe or know about an object can neither be considered to be properties of that object nor things which can be true of that object, at least for the purposes of identity statements. It is not a real property of a thing that I know, perceive or believe something about it. So long as we don't make the mistake of counting these truths among the real properties of a thing, Leibniz's Law holds.

How does this apply to the argument for dualism? The argument for dualism depends upon the fact that mind and matter have different properties. But if we look back at our list, how many of these are genuine properties of mind and matter, and how many are more accurately described as features of how we think about or perceive them? For instance, it may be false that minds are not in space. It may just be that we don't perceive them spatially. In fact, in some sense minds do seem to be in time and space. I think mine's somewhere behind my eyes right now! Where's yours?

Similar doubts can be cast on all the other apparent real differences between mind and body. The fact that minds are private is simply a result of the different perspectives we have on minds and matter, not a result of the nature of minds. Telepathic people would not think minds were private, so if telepathy is even conceivable, mind is not necessarily private.

The fact that we cannot be wrong about states of our own minds, but can be wrong about matter clearly concerns what we know about mind and matter, not how they actually are. So this may not be a real difference in properties. (It is also possible to argue that we just can be wrong about the states of our minds. We may think we feel righteous indignation when we really feel jealousy, for example.)

Each set of apparently different properties can be treated in a similar way. Of course, it is a matter of debate whether any of these are real properties or not. You may still think some are. But the case has to be made in the light of the lessons of the masked man fallacy.

One of the most powerful arguments against dualism is found in Gilbert Ryle's classic *The Concept of Mind* (1949). Ryle believed that the argument for dualism rests upon what he calls a category mistake. A category mistake is where you put something under one category when it should come under another. Historically, there have been two main philosophical categories: substance (stuff) and attribute (size, shape, colour and other characteristics described by adjectives). Even within each category there are different sub-categories. Not all nouns refer to things in the same way. For example, if you want to see Oxford University, I have to show you all the different colleges and buildings which make up the University. Although the University is clearly not any one of these things, nor is it another thing additional to all these parts. The University is not in the same category of existence as all the individual institutions that make up the University. Another of Ryle's examples is of the foreigner who watches a cricket match, and sees who bowls, bats and fields, but doesn't see who contributes the team spirit. Contributing team spirit is simply not the same kind of thing as fulfilling a single function. It is the difference between doing an action and the way you do an action.

The problem with the argument for dualism is that it says mind is not the same as matter and concludes that it must be a different kind of substance to matter. But isn't it more correct to conclude that the mind just isn't a substance at all? Calling it a substance is simply to put it into the wrong category. Just because the mind cannot be described as physical stuff that doesn't mean it has to be described as some other kind of stuff.

If we look back at the argument for dualism, we can see that the conclusion was just that mind is not the same as matter. Interpreting this as meaning that mind and matter are two different substances required an extra step. This step is not taken by property dualism. On this view, mind and matter are two different attributes of one substance. In other words, there are not two 'stuffs' – mind and matter – but one stuff which has mental and physical properties. Neither of these properties is more fundamental than the other and neither can be explained in terms of the other. So you can understand things as physical or as mental, but not as both at the same time.

Property dualism is attractive as it preserves the intuitive difference between mind and matter without leading to the implausibilities of substance dualism. But it is not without its own difficulties. In particular, it seems that mind is a property of relatively few things in the universe. But if property dualism is correct, everything has both mental and physical properties. But in what sense does a stone have mental properties?

Arguments about dualism may be inconclusive. But when deciding whether to accept it as true, we don't only need to consider these arguments. We also need to consider rival views and how plausible they are. So we need to move on to examine a few of them.

▶ Behaviourism

The picture dualism paints of the private self, hidden within the public body, seems to lead us to an insoluble problem. Mental events are supposed to be by their very nature private, only directly observable by the person who has them, whereas physical events are said to be public. But if mental events are indeed private, then how can we meaningfully talk about them or know other people have them? (See the section on other minds.) Dualism creates two worlds – the inner and the outer – and leaves unexplained the link between them.

Behaviourism attempts to solve this problem by claiming that mental concepts do not refer to private, inner events at all, but to public events. In other words, it defines psychological functioning in terms of observed behaviour. We do not need to talk about what goes on 'inside our heads' at all. All we need talk about is behaviour. By behaviour we should mean any publicly observable event, be it behaviour in the ordinary sense of the word or in the sense of the physical behaviour of matter.

Behaviourism comes in two main varieties and varying strengths. Methodological behaviourism belongs in psychology, and is basically a means of doing psychology solely based on observation of behaviour (rather than relying on introspection), with the aim of making the discipline more scientific. The major philosophical variety is logical behaviourism, which claims that everything mental is either a behavioural state, or a disposition to behave in a certain way. So, for example, to be in pain is to be unable to comfortably use the part of the body in pain, to tend to grimace, bite your lip or scream if prodded and so on. To be impatient is to tend to act in an impatient way more often than is usual.

Behaviourism often appears barmy, because it seems to talk about mental states as if they didn't exist. To talk of pain without talking about the sensation one feels seems to miss the point. But behaviourists do not all deny we have such sensations. Weak behaviourists claim that although psychological concepts refer to behaviour that does not mean that there are no such things as inner sensations. It is just that they have no part to play in the meaning of mental terms. Only strong behaviourists claim there are no such things as sensations and consciousness. This view seems to require us to 'feign anaesthesia'.

If you think behaviourism is crazy, ask yourself this: could you ascribe a mental life to someone on anything other than behavioural grounds? If the answer is no, you are beginning to see the appeal of behaviourism. If all we need to know to ascribe a mind to someone is behavioural information, then why should we believe that mental concepts refer to something else unconnected with behaviour?

We have seen what behaviourism is, but not arguments for it. One argument takes up Ryle's argument about how dualists made a category mistake by placing the mental under the category of substance. So what is the right category for the mental? Ryle thought that the mental is a complexity of performances, in other words, of behaviours. Most of *The Concept of Mind* is spent accounting for every mental occurrence under the sun in terms of behaviour. For example, 'to know something' is not to be in possession of some hidden idea, or an inner piece of knowledge, but to be able to speak correctly about the thing, recognise it when you see it, tell it from a hawk or a handsaw and so on. Ryle also distinguishes between occurrences, which are individual events, and dispositions, which are tendencies to perform such occurrences. For example, saying something clever is an occurrence, and being clever is the disposition to perform many such occurrences. In neither case is there a need to talk about the inner self or soul.

Ryle's argument is not a deductive, but an inductive one. He claims dualism leads to intractable difficulties and it mistakenly takes mind to be a substance. That is his negative case against dualism. His positive case is simply that behaviourism provides an alternative 'one-world theory', which is preferable to the two worlds of dualism. This theory not only makes the mental explicable, but it also accounts for how we are able to know that others think and to explain our mental lives in the first place. We can do these things because the mental is as public as the local library.

A second route to behaviourism comes from logical positivism. The logical positivists were a collection of early twentieth-century philosophers who thought too much philosophy was airy nonsense. They sought to distinguish sense from nonsense and thought they had found a way of so doing in the principle of verification. This is the principle that statements are only meaningful if they can be verified either (directly or indirectly) by sense experiences or by their logical relation to other words and concepts. The former is the way matters of fact are settled and the latter matters of logic. So, for example, 'The world is controlled by undetectable green Martians' is meaningless because nothing could count as evidence for or against it, whilst 'Tony Blair is a weatherman' is meaningful, though untrue, because we know what would have to be the case for it to be true and it isn't the case. The logical positivists hoped that this principle would help rid philosophy of all nonsense.

How does this lead to behaviourism? Well, what would count as evidence for a person being in a mental state such as pain? Here's a list: they say they are; they roll around on the floor; C-fibres are stimulated in their brains; they don't want to play rugby; they have a knife sticking out of their knee. You can think of many more. The point is, 'they are feeling a sensation' doesn't come into it. It can't count as evidence because if it exists, it's unobservable. So, there may be inner sensations, but they have no role to play in the meaning of mental concepts. The only way of talking about the mental which makes sense turns out to be talk about behaviour.

Behaviourism has its attractions, most notably in the way in which it demystifies the mind. It makes it clear just how it is we are able to talk about the mind, because it destroys that idea of the mind as private and inner – what Ryle called 'the pernicious myth of the ghost in the machine'.

It also provides us with a test for consciousness: If something behaves like a thinking thing, it is a thinking thing. Since our mental vocabulary refers only to behaviour, if a machine or another being behaves in a way consistent with consciousness, we must say it is conscious. We cannot demand it behaves in the right way and in addition is conscious, as there is simply nothing additional to behaviour which constitutes consciousness. We believe other people are conscious because of their behaviour. Therefore, we would also have to attribute consciousness to robots or aliens if they behaved in the appropriate way. Otherwise, we would be demanding a standard of proof not only higher than the one we apply to ourselves, but also arguably higher than it is possible to meet. For what other test of consciousness is there other than behaviour?

▶ Arguments against behaviourism

Many people claim behaviourism fails because it leaves out the defining feature of mind: 'qualia'. Qualia are the ways things feel or appear to us. In Thomas Nagel's terminology, there is 'something it is like' to feel pain or to see a colour, and this is not accounted for by behaviourists.

One obvious reply to this is that a weak behaviourist would not deny qualia exist, but would only claim they have no part to play in the meaning of 'mind'. This may not be an adequate response. First, how can the defining feature of a thing not be essential to what that thing means? This seems a contradiction. Second, surely the behaviourist would have to claim that the very term qualia was meaningless or irrelevant. For example, the logical positivist would view the claim that there are such things as qualia as unverifiable, and thus meaningless nonsense we should not discuss. Hence, the behaviourist must insist that we cannot talk about the one thing that seems essential to mind, which is hard to swallow.

But it's worse than this. Is there any logical contradiction in imagining a mental state with no behavioural manifestations? Surely not. What are the behavioural manifestation of imagining a square, or dreaming whilst in a coma? The behaviourist could just bite the bullet and say a mental event without a behavioural manifestation is impossible, but they would have to give some pretty good reasons to persuade us this is true given the apparently obvious counter-examples.

One objection which is less persuasive is that behaviourism would not be able to draw a distinction between, for example, acting being in pain and actually being in pain. In fact, the behaviourist can account for that difference. If a person is acting being in pain, there are circumstances in which the truth would out, where they would behave in a way inconsistent with their really being in pain. To say someone is in pain is not just to say something about their actual behaviour, but how they would behave in other circumstances. We may not be able to actually trip someone up, but this only shows they are good actors, not that they are in pain.

Apart from these general objections to behaviourism, we can also criticise the particular arguments which are used to establish it. As concerns Ryle's argument, it is enough to point out that, although he may be right to say the dualists have put mind in the wrong category, he may have also been wrong to characterise it in terms of behaviour. Given the difficulties such a categorisation makes, as shown above, this may seem a fair criticism.

The logical positivist's main problem is that the principle of verification is a very dubious one. The main reason for saying this is that the principle itself is not verifiable, so by its own criteria it is meaningless! Hence, it can be shown to be self-defeating. Second, how far can we stretch the idea that something need only be verifiable in principle? Although it seems true that we can't verify statements concerning private mental events, that seems to be a contingent not necessary fact. Were we telepathic – and this seems a logical possibility – we could observe other minds as easily as we could other bodies, and so verification would be possible. This seems consistent with the claim that meaningful statements are in principle verifiable.

The behaviourists certainly seem to have hit upon something when they say talk of the mental is based on behaviour, but perhaps they go too far when they claim the mental is nothing but behaviour. Even if we reject behaviourism, we should thank it for reminding us of how much of what we say about 'the private' is in fact perfectly explicable in terms of 'the public'.

▶ Physicalism

Physicalists claim that mind is brain and they support this claim by arguing that it is an empirical hypothesis for which there is overwhelming evidence. Supporters of this theory have thus to do two things: First, show the evidence that supports it and, second, show that the philosophical barriers to accepting the theory are illusory.

First, the evidence. Exhibit A is simply the huge problems caused by supposing there are two substances in the world: mind and matter. Dualists have never given a convincing explanation of how they interact. What's more, there is no reason why postulating a second substance – mind – makes the existence of mental states any easier to understand. Given that there is nothing to gain from claiming there is a mental substance, and quite a lot to lose, applying the principle of Ockham's Razor (that we should not postulate the existence of more entities than is necessary), we should accept a monist view that there is only one substance: matter. And so our minds also must be made of matter.

Exhibit B is also based on Ockham's Razor, but focuses on the successes of science rather than the failures of dualism. As Smart put it, it just seems inconceivable that everything in the universe is made up of complex arrangements of physical matter and is explicable in scientific terms – except minds. The principle of Ockham's Razor suggests that, if possible, we should account for the universe in terms of only one type of entity, and considering that we can explain so much physically, it would be more natural to consider the mind as physical than it would to suggest the world is mental.

Exhibit C moves from science's general success to particular findings about the mind. Experiments show that mind and brain are intimately connected. We could believe that there is simply a correlation between the mental and the physical. But then, how would this correlation be explained? Again, isn't it simpler and easier to say that in place of a correlation, there is in fact an identity between mind and body? The reason why C-fibres fire in my brain when I feel pain is not because pain and C-fibres are correlated, but because C-fibre stimulation and pain are the same thing. Consider this analogy: you don't have to be Sherlock Holmes to work out that if everywhere the Prime Minister is, Tony Blair is there too, to realise that Tony Blair is the Prime Minister.

The problem for physicalism is that there seem to be many philosophical barriers to accepting the theory. One is that because we can conceive of artificial intelligence and aliens with minds, mind cannot be the same thing as brain. This is because neither computers nor aliens would have brains, as 'brain' refers to a bit of earth biology. This is not a fatal objection, because physicalism does not claim that the identity is necessary, but contingent. Minds could conceivably be other things, but in our case they are brains. So when physicalism claims minds are brains, it does not deny that they could have been, or elsewhere could be, other things. That mind happens to be brain is a contingent truth, just as the fact that Blair is the Prime Minister of Britain in 2001 is contingent.

Some argue that mind can't be brain, because the meaning of the words are completely different. If mind was brain, they would mean the same thing, but as we have known what mind is for centuries without knowing it is mind, this is impossible. But saying that a mental state is identical with a brain state does not mean that 'brain' and 'mental' mean the same thing. Consider the example of how lightning is identical with an electrical discharge. This does not mean that 'lightning' and 'electrical discharge' mean the same thing. We have to distinguish the *extension* and *intension* of a noun. The extension of a noun is those things which the noun applies to. The extension of the word 'tiger' is all the tigers that there are. However, the intension of a noun is the definitional meaning the word has. The definitional meaning of the word 'tiger' is something like, 'a particular kind of feline indigenous to India'. Although 'lightning' and 'electrical discharge' do not have the same intension, they do have the same extension. It is the extension of the nouns which is held to be identical. So it is with mind and body.

For similar reasons, the objection that mind and brain are logically distinct (i.e. you can't deduce facts about one from facts about the other) doesn't hold water. J. J. C. Smart also claims that the logics of mind statements and body statements are distinct. Using his analogy, a nation is identical with its citizens, but the logics of nation statements and citizen statements are different. You can't directly translate facts about one to the other, but that does not mean that nations are anything over and above their citizens.

To sum up, in philosophical jargon, mind and brain may mean different things (be semantically distinct) and not be logically equivalent (be logically distinct), but still be the same thing (ontologically identical).

However, these logical and semantic objections do not exhaust physicalism's difficulties. The most serious are yet to come. The starting point is that it seems we cannot deny that there are irreducible mental properties. By this we mean that there are features of the mental, in particular qualia, which cannot be explained in physical terms. 'What it is like' to have a mind is not part of physics, but it is an essential part of the mental. So, if physicalism is to be credible, it must allow space for qualia and consciousness. Many have argued that it cannot do so, because the claim that mind just is matter is shattered as soon as you accept that there are mental properties, as matter can only have physical properties. Hence, physicalism seems to miss something out.

One solution would be to bite the bullet and become an eliminative materialist, like Paul Churchland, and simply deny there are any mental properties or qualia. There are very intelligent people who believe this, but rather like the strong behaviourists, it is hard to be convinced by them or see how they can claim there is no such thing as an inner mental life. The other alternative is to allow the existence of irreducible mental properties, but still claim that mind is brain. Mental features can be explained as merely the way in which brain appears to us, as a kind of by-product. This is a tricky position to hold. We feel that it is because of our conscious thoughts that we act. It is our decisions which cause action. But physicalism seems to undermine this. It claims brain processes cause action, and the feeling of making a decision has nothing to do with it. As Searle put it, it is as though, the froth on the sea were to think, 'gee, pulling these waves back and forth is really hard work!', where froth is to consciousness what sea is to brain. This seems to make consciousness an epiphenomenon, that is a phenomenon which just 'sits' above brain without causing any of what goes on.

Why is epiphenomenalism supposed to be such a bad thing? One reason is that it undermines our feeling that we are free. If consciousness is just an epiphenomenon, then we are certainly not free. That is a consequence of the view, but doesn't seem to be a good objection, as many philosophers agree that we are not free. The second reason is that if mind is an epiphenomenon, then why does it exist? Why would we have been given or evolved consciousness if it has no part to play in our lives? Whether you're a determinist or not, surely consciousness must have a role.

One reply would be to say that thoughts do play a part in the causal story, because thoughts are just brain events, and these cause actions. But this isn't good enough, because it doesn't give the conscious feature of brain events a role to play. In fact, it is very hard to see how a physicalist could say that consciousness – an irreducible mental property – has a role in causation if mind is just a physical thing, a brain.

Despite the doubts, physicalism has got to be on to something. The link between mind and brain is not just close, it's intimate. The claim that there can be no thought without brain activity is as sound a scientific claim as any. But there do seem to be real, insurmountable problems with drawing the conclusion from this that mind is identical to brain.

▶ Functionalism

Philosophy is often criticised for its lack of progress, but there has at least been development in the philosophy of mind, and we can see functionalism as a theory which learns from past theories and their mistakes. If we survey dualism, behaviourism and physicalism, what could we actually agree about? Here's a suggested list:

The lesson of dualism is that the claim that mind and brain are distinct substances is misguided and wrong.
The lesson of behaviourism is that the basis of our understanding of mind is what is publicly observable.
The lesson of physicalism is that, given what we have found out, we must find a place for brain in our discussion of the mind.
And a general lesson is that we must not leave out consciousness or qualia from our account of mind.

Functionalism builds on these insights and adds one of its own: given that artificial intelligence appears to be a real possibility, our concept of mind must provide us with a means of detecting minds in things other than ourselves. Functionalism can trace its roots back to mathematician Alan Turing's famous test. The Turing Test is a way of seeing whether a machine can think or not. If it is able to produce outputs in response to inputs which are indistinguishable from those of a person, then it is intelligent. Hence, a thing has a mind if it is able to produce 'intelligent' outputs. This, in a nutshell, is functionalism.

Functionalists believe this theory meets all the criteria of a credible theory of mind. First, it does not require a special, mental substance. Second, it bases the concept of mind on what is public, observable and within our own experience. Third, it gives a role to brain. It is clearly because we have brains that we are able to produce intelligent outputs, so even if it is not true that mind is brain, the fact that we have a mind is largely, if not entirely, down to our having brains. Fourth, it gives us a test for the having of a mind that we can apply equally to humans and other beings or machines. The problem of other minds is thus dissolved. Fifth, it allows room for qualia and consciousness, because it doesn't tell us everything about the nature of a particular mind, it only says what a system must do to have a mind. The test for having a mind is functioning, but then the mind in question may have other features as well, such as sensations.

Functionalism is often confused with behaviourism. But there is one important difference. The behaviourist says mind is no more than behaviour. Being in a mental state is being in a behavioural state. Functionalists, however, do not say a mind is the inputs and outputs, but rather that the mind is what receives inputs and produces outputs. Because any number of things may be able to function in such a way, and they may all have different internal structures, there is scope for different kinds of minds. The qualia of our minds are thus just a feature of our minds, rather than an essential feature of minds.

Functionalism flourished for a while, but there is one major objection against it. Searle's famous Chinese room argument is a powerful critique of functionalism. (It also works against behaviourism, arguably even better.) His argument is aimed at destroying the main claim of functionalism that anything that has the appropriate input–output relations has a mind.

Searle's objection can be summed up in an aphorism: it is a consequence of functionalism that if we could arrange a load of beer cans to accept inputs and produce outputs in the right way, then according to the functionalist it would have a mind. Searle thinks this is absurd, but this is not much of an argument, because the functionalist would be happy to accept this consequence, and would simply ask why Searle is so threatened by the idea of thinking beer cans.

Searle can back up his vivid beer can objection with an argument. It does not show that a computer could not think, or that artificial intelligence is impossible, but that a digital computer (the kind of computer we currently have) could never think, and his explanation of why it couldn't raises serious problems for the functionalist.

The argument hinges on the difference between semantics and syntax. Syntax concerns the formal rules for the construction of sentences in language, whilst semantics concerns meaning. A computer is a purely syntactical system. It follows rules but that is all it does. Searle argues that it is impossible for a purely syntactical system ever to also have semantics, that is to say meaning. His argument for this is simple.

Imagine a room, in which there is a man, a guidebook and a lot of Chinese characters. A series of Chinese characters are sent into the room. The man inside then looks through his guidebook, follows instructions to arrange other Chinese symbols into sequences and then passes these out of the room. Unbeknown to the man, who has no knowledge of Chinese, the symbols he receives are questions, and those he sends out are answers. It is clear that the Chinese room is functioning like a system which understands Chinese. It is also clear that no understanding of Chinese is required at any stage of the process. It is also clear that there is no way in which, from this process alone, the man can come to understand what the Chinese symbols mean. This demonstrates that functioning is not a sufficient criterion for having a mind because semantics cannot arise in a purely syntactical system. A digital computer, as it is basically a syntactical system which operates merely by manipulating symbols according to set rules, is thus just like the Chinese room, and so it is clear that a digital computer could not think, as thinking requires semantics.

One objection to this argument is that, although it is true that the man in the room doesn't understand Chinese, the system as a whole – man, book, symbols and room – does. It could be argued that the brain is like this. One cannot point to a part of the brain which understands, but none the less, the brain as a whole does.

Searle rejects this objection. The basic point still stands – the system as a whole is a syntactical one, and one cannot get from syntax to semantics. To suppose otherwise is merely to presume functionalism. There is no other good reason to say that the room as a whole thinks.

A further objection is that if the room were not a room, but a kind of robot interacting with the world, then it would think. Searle is not convinced. It just doesn't seem relevant to the question how sophisticated, mobile or interactive the system is. If it works on pure syntax, no matter how much we get it to function like a thinking thing, it won't be a thinking thing.

Searle's argument is a strong one, but it raises several questions. First, what grounds other than functioning do we have to go on in order to decide whether a system is conscious or not? Searle may not be able to provide a positive answer to this, but he could maintain that if we know a system is only syntactical, we can know it doesn't think. In other cases, we simply may not be able to say.

Second, isn't it possible that semantics is an emergent quality? In other words, could it not be true that consciousness begins to arise as a result of increasing sophistication in a syntactical system? If not, from where does consciousness arise? Searle need not answer this second question, but his argument certainly seems to rule out the first possibility without any real justification.

One further difficulty is simply that functionalism cannot distinguish between a system which simulates thought and one that produces it. Surely, there must actually be a difference between the two, but functionalism doesn't account for it.

***

Dualism, behaviourism, physicalism and functionalism all have their problems. Versions of functionalism remain the most popular in Anglo-American philosophy departments, but there is no winner in this race yet. The philosophy of mind is a very active area in philosophy and increasingly philosophers are trying to solve the mind–body problem in an interdisciplinary way, working with neurologists and psychologists.

There is more to the philosophy of mind, however, than these four theories of what mind is. Another issue is the problem of other minds.

▶ Other minds

Put in its strongest form, the problem of other minds is: 'How can we know whether other beings have minds?' However, given that it seems impossible to prove that other people have minds, but we do believe that they have, a more modest question is: 'How can we justify our statements and beliefs about other minds?'

Why is there a problem about other minds at all? What seems to make them 'unknowable'? Our knowledge extends to everything which is part of the perceptible world. But how things appear to others, how things feel and so on (what Russell calls the 'qualitative character' of the world), is not included in this arena of knowledge. Therefore, it seems that we can know only the objective facts about other people and nothing of how the world appears to them or of the character of their thought.

It is also widely believed that people's thoughts and sensations are necessarily private, that they just cannot be inspected by others. If this is true, then it is clear that only the person who has the thoughts and sensations can directly observe them.

Strong physicalism could resolve this problem. If, say, a pain is a brain process, then observing the brain process would be observing a pain. However, we would still not be able to observe the *qualitative character* of the pain. This would remain private. And as the mind–brain identity is contingent, there is always the possibility that any particular brain state is not the mind state it was thought to be.

There are several interesting arguments about the problem of other minds in the writings of Bertrand Russell and A. J. Ayer. Russell put forward one solution to the problem: the argument from analogy. Because other people's behaviour resembles our own, and our behaviour is accompanied by mental processes, we assume that other people also have these processes. For example, if I report a pain, it is because I have a certain unpleasant experience. If someone else reports a pain, I assume that they too are having an unpleasant experience.

As it stands the argument is weak. As Ayer explains: if I lived in a society where no-one ever appeared naked, and I had a hidden birthmark, I would not be justified in assuming that everyone else had a similar birthmark. Similarly, to generalise from only my own case that other people also have thoughts is not a justifiable inference.

Ayer also rejects a behaviour-based version of the analogy argument. We learn what words like 'pain' mean by observing the behaviour of others. Hence, our justification for attributing pain to them simply comes from the fact that their behaviour exemplifies what pain means. In this way, 'pain' doesn't refer to a particular type of inner sensation at all. Rather, pain is *whatever* causes a certain type of behaviour. And so if that behaviour is present, then pain must also be present, as pain is simply the cause of the behaviour. In this way, the problem of other minds is dissolved.

Ayer argues that this is wrong, because he sees no reason to suppose that the meaning of words should be strictly determined by the way in which they were learned. In other words, just because we learn what mind-words mean by observing behaviour, it doesn't mean that the meanings of these words are exhausted by what can be observed in behaviour. The mistake here is to confuse the method of learning a word with its actual meaning. I might learn what a tiger is by seeing photos, for example, but it doesn't follow that 'tiger' means 'photo of a tiger'. In the same way, it doesn't follow from the fact that we learn about mental concepts from behaviour that the manifestation of certain kinds of behaviours ensures that which the mental concepts refer to are present.

The argument from analogy refuses to go away, however. It just gets more complex. Russell argued that the general form of the argument from analogy is that we observe in ourselves that 'A causes B', where A is a mental occurrence and B a physical occurrence. For instance, a mental occurrence such as the sensation of pain causes a physical shriek. However, we sometimes observe in others a B (for example, a shriek) when we do not observe an A (for example, a painful sensation). In these cases, we simply assume that there is an A which is the cause of B, only we can't observe it. (Consider how when we see David Copperfield 'flying', we assume there is a string causing this action, even though we cannot see it.)

However, to justify this inference, we need to know that *only* A causes B, or that most Bs are caused by As. If not, then it is more than possible that the observed physical occurrence is caused by an unobserved, but not mental occurrence. Even though we are still only generalising from our own cases, we do in fact make this assumption.

Ayer, however, is not convinced. That A causes B in us is still a very flimsy basis on which to infer that this is true of everyone else. Russell may have explained what the assumptions are that govern our belief in other minds very well, but he is still only describing an assumption, not providing an argument.

Is there no solution to the problem of other minds then? Ayer thinks there is and endorses that of Hilary Putnam. Putnam argues that the belief that other people have minds like mine is justified because it explains human behaviour. What is more, there is no other rival theory which explains human behaviour so well. The postulate of other minds is part of a wider theory (not a scientific theory, but a practical theory) which accounts for the behaviour of people by attributing conscious thoughts to them. This theory just has no credible rival. Put simply, we are justified in believing in other minds because no rival theory even gets close to explaining why other people behave as they do.

The problem with the problem of other minds is that, like all sceptical problems, it is impossible to prove beyond all doubt that other people do have minds. It is always possible that we are wrong to ascribe minds to others (see Chapter 1 on the theory of knowledge). The way out of the problem may be to accept that a full proof is just unattainable and demanding one is inappropriate. As Aristotle once said: 'It is the mark of the trained mind never to expect more precision in the treatment of any subject than the nature of that subject permits.'

▶ Personal identity

Minds matter to us because having a mind is the hallmark of being a person. This is why the puzzle of mind is so important to the issue of personal identity. The philosophical problem of personal identity can be expressed in the question: 'What are the necessary and sufficient conditions for a person A at one time being the same person as person B at another time?'

The arguments of the dualists, and René Descartes in particular, favoured the view that continuity of the self depends on the continuity of a mental substance or soul. It follows from the arguments for dualism that a person's essence is an indivisible, immaterial thinking thing. As this is the essence of a person, it seems clear that this and this alone is required for a person to continue to exist.

All the objections given against dualism also apply against this view of personal identity. But there is one crucial objection offered by Locke which aims to show that, even if dualism is true, personal identity doesn't depend on the continued existence of the soul. He offers a thought experiment:

> Let anyone reflect upon himself and conclude that he has in himself an imma-terial spirit, which is that which thinks in him and in the constant change of his body keeps him the same. Let him also suppose it to be the same soul that was in Nestor or Thersites at the siege of Troy, but he now having no consciousness of any of the actions either of Nestor or Thersites, does he or can he conceive himself to be the same person with either of them? Can he be concerned in either of their actions, attribute them to himself, or think of them as his own, more than the actions of any other men that ever existed?
>
> (*An Essay concerning Human Understanding*, Book 2)

Locke's point is simple. He invites us to imagine that we share the same soul as a person who previously existed. This is entirely possible, if dualism is true. But if we don't remember what that person did, and if their plans are not our plans, in other words, if there is no mental link between us and them, we can't be them, even though we have the same soul.

This is not so much an argument as a way of making some key intuitions about persons clear to us. If Locke is right, the continued existence of the soul, even if it exists, is not a sufficient condition for personal identity over time. Further, it suggests that the key factor in personal identity is continuity of consciousness. This is the key idea of the theory of personal identity known as psychological reductionism.

We are all familiar with the fantasy idea of waking up in another person's body, or being 'beamed up', *Star Trek* style. What is it about these fantasies that convince us that the person who wakes up in another body or on Mars is us? It is the fact that the person would think they were us, that they would have the same personality, plans and memories as us.

The most prominent contemporary proponent of this theory is Derek Parfit. He offers a compelling thought experiment to demonstrate the point in which he imagines what it is like to be teletransported across space to Mars. This process may involve destroying the original body and creating a new one from different matter. Even though the Parfit on Mars has a body that shares not a single cell with the Parfit on Earth, and certainly hasn't got the same soul, it seems right to say that Parfit has made the journey to Mars. This is because there is what Parfit calls psychological connectedness and continuity between Earth-Parfit and Mars-Parfit. This view is hence called psychological reduction-ism because it reduces all the factors that normally accompany survival, especially bodily continuity, down to what it considers essential – psychological continuity.

Locke's version of the thesis came under attack because it was thought (wrongly) that his only criterion for personal identity is continuity of memory. In other words:

Peter 1 on 1/1/97 is the same person as Peter 2 on 2/1/97 if and only if Peter 2 remembers enough of Peter 1's experiences.

We say *enough* of Peter 1's experiences because we do not expect someone to remember everything over time. As this stands this is neither sufficient nor necessary for personal identity. It is not sufficient because if it were possible that another person could, through mind-reading, come to be aware of all your memories, they would clearly not then be you. It is not necessary for a more subtle reason. It is a law of logic that:

If X = Y and X = Z then Y = Z

For example, if the teacher is Bertie and the teacher is an axe murderer, then Bertie is an axe murderer. Consider what happens when we apply this principle of logic and the memory criterion for personal identity to a case like this:

There is a young boy (YB) who stole some apples, who grew up to be a soldier (S) who saved a comrade, who grew up to be an old major (OM). The wartime hero remembered stealing the apples. The old major has forgotten about his wartime exploits but remembers stealing the apples.

What would the memory criterion say about this? It would say that YB is S, and that YB is OM, because there are memory connections between them. But then it would say S is not OM, because there are no memory connections between them. But this contradicts the law of logic stated above: If YB = S and YB = OM then S = OM. Because the memory criterion denies S = OM, which is surely true, the memory criterion must be wrong.

That is not the end of the road for psychological reductionists, though. They tend to say that memory alone is not enough: there also have to be connections of intention, personality, dispositions, preferences and so on. Of course, these factors all change over time, but as long as there is an evolving change, without sudden, drastic change, then there is psychological continuity and hence personal identity.

The real problem for this view comes in a continuation to the Mars story started above. Parfit imagines entering the teleterporter one day, only to find that he has been 'sent' to Mars, but not destroyed on Earth. There is now both an Earth-Parfit and Mars-Parfit. In this case, the person on Mars is psychologically continuous with the person on Earth, but he is clearly not that person, as the Earth person is still on Earth. He is best described as a clone. But if he is a clone in this situation, and he would be no different if the Earth person *had* been destroyed, then he must be a clone whatever happens. So it seems that psychological continuity is not enough for personal identity. It may simply result in a clone.

Such worries have led some people to think that the whole debate has gone horribly wrong. What we have failed to recognise, they say, is that we are essentially animals. Sure, you can have psychological continuity, and some people wouldn't want to go on living without it, but if we're talking about identity, the only thing that is necessary and sufficient is continuity of bodily existence. This view is known as animalism.

This view requires an immediate modification. We know people can continue to live with transplanted and synthetic organs and limbs. So what if we could be entirely replaced by such body parts? Isn't this compatible with survival?

Because of this, most defenders of this view would say that the crucial organ is the brain, as this controls thought. Everything else could be replaced, but not the brain.

However, if they admit that the brain is vital because it carries consciousness, why not admit that consciousness is what is important, not the brain which just happens to be the carrier of consciousness? This would lead back to psychological reductionism. A second problem is to ask why the brain can't be replaced by synthetic parts anyway? Why is it okay to transplant hearts and legs, but not okay to transplant brains? So long as the brain was able to continue a person's mental life, what's the problem?

This is a long-running and difficult debate where people have strong gut instincts. All the views considered have something going for them, but all seem to have something wrong too. Perhaps the problem lies in a confusion over the question. Is the issue a factual one concerning identity, or is it a question of value, concerning what we would consider to be an acceptable future? If it is the former, then maybe it should be answered in the same way as we answer questions about other organisms, and so the animalist would be going along the right lines. If it is the latter, then perhaps a mixed view, with key elements of the psychological reductionist position is more fruitful. How you decide will perhaps reveal a lot about what you value in your own existence.

▶ Conclusion

Almost everyone now agrees that mind is somehow made possible in humans by the functioning of our brains. Yet the study of brains is still in its infancy. There is still so much we have to learn about it. The philosophy of mind, however, has been carried out for centuries without even this basic knowledge about brains. Given that, one might think it remarkable that the subject has progressed at all. While it does seem true to say that the philosophy of mind has taught us a great deal, we should perhaps accept that the solutions to the big problems will only come when we understand better how the brain works. Philosophy has done its best to understand mind but some problems will take greater scientific knowledge to really solve.

Summary

The main question in the philosophy of mind concerns the mind's relation to matter and, in particular, to the body. Why is it that we do not seem able to understand mind in terms of the movement of physical matter when it seems everything else in the universe can be explained in this way?

Dualism's answer is that mind and body, since they have two very different sets of properties, are two different kinds of substance. The main problem with this theory is explaining how two so very different things could interact, especially since it seems true that mind and matter causally interact with each other.

Behaviourists argue that all mental concepts refer not to private, non-material things and events, but to publicly observable behaviours or dispositions to behave. The main problem with this view is that not all mental states have some kind of behavioural manifestation.

Physicalism is the view that any mental event is identical with some physical event, which in the case of humans will be a brain event. The reason that a brain event doesn't seem to be the same kind of thing as a mental event is simply that there are two ways of experiencing it – from the 'inside' and from the 'outside'. The major difficulty for physicalism is explaining how brain events and mental events can be the same when they seem to have such radically different properties.

Functionalists argue something has a mind if it is capable of processing inputs and producing outputs in an intelligent way. It is neutral as to what kind of thing, organic or silicon, does this and what it feels like to be such a mind. The major objection to functionalism comes from Searle's Chinese Room argument, which attempts to shows that a functionalist system could be just a rule-following device with none of the understanding required for intelligence.

The problem of other minds is the problem of how we can know other people have minds when we cannot know they have an inner life – we can only observe their behaviour. One solution is the argument from analogy, which says that we attribute mental states to others because they resemble us in key respects. We ourselves have minds, so it seems reasonable to attribute mental states to others too. Putnam's solution is that the hypothesis that others do have minds is simply the best explanation for why they behave as they do.

The problem of personal identity concerns what it is that makes a person the same person over time, given all the changes a person may undergo. A traditional view is that personal identity is determined by the continued existence of a non-physical soul. Psychological reductionists claim personal identity is a matter of psychological connectedness and continuity. Animalists claim personal identity is simply the continued existence of a particular human animal.

Glossary

Category mistake   To think of one kind of thing or phenomenon as though it were a different kind of thing or phenomenon. For example, to think of a university as a kind of building rather than an institution.

Identity   Strict identity means that if X is identical to Y, all and only the properties of X are properties of Y.

Logical behaviourism   The view that all mental concepts refer to behaviours or dispositions to behave.

Mental   Everything that is characteristic of conscious beings, such as thoughts, sense perceptions and emotions.

Methodological behaviourism   The view that the best way to study the mind is to study behaviour.

Monism   The view that there is only one substance, rather than the two postulated by substance dualism.

Physical   All that is the subject of the physical sciences.

Property dualism   The view that things have two different kinds of properties – mental and physical – even though they are made of just one substance.

Qualia   The way experiences feel to conscious beings. 'What it feels like' to have a thought, perception, emotion and so on.

Qualitative identity   The sense in which two objects, though distinct entities, can be called identical because they share all the same properties except their location in time and space.

Quantitative identity   The kind of identity where two apparently different things are in fact one and the same thing.

Semantics   Meaning in language.

Substance dualism   The view that there are two different kinds of substance, the mental and the physical.

Syntax   The formal rules which govern the construction of sentences.

Further reading

The classic exposition of dualism is René Descartes's *Meditations on First Philosophy*, which is one of the books covered in the companion volume to this one,

Philosophy: Key Texts. A devastating critique of the Cartesian view and a major work for behaviourism is Gilbert Ryle's *The Concept of Mind* (Penguin), which is a lucid read.

A brilliant anthology of academic philosophy and weird sci-fi is *The Mind's I*, edited by Douglas R. Hofstadter and Daniel C. Dennett (Penguin). It contains many fascinating riffs on functionalist themes as well as covering a lot of other ground. John Searle's *Minds, Brains and Science* (Penguin) is a very readable précis of Searle's own work in the area. Tim Crane's *The Mechanical Mind* (Penguin) is a very clear and informative book which brings the debate right up to date.

Personal Identity, edited by John Perry (University of California Press), is an authoritative but select set of readings on the theme of the title. It includes Parfit's original paper on personal identity. For an original take on the problem of other minds, try Simon Glendinning's *Being with Others* (Routledge).

4 Philosophy of Religion

▶ What is the philosophy of religion?

The philosophy of religion is largely concerned with the rational grounds for belief or non-belief in God. It differs from theology in that theology starts from a particular religious belief or set of beliefs and seeks to understand and explore questions in religion from that starting point. The philosophy of religion, on the other hand, is not supposed to start with any assumptions or prior beliefs. Its goal is to examine the basis of religious belief and to do that it cannot assume that any religious beliefs are true or false.

In practice this distinction between the philosophy of religion and theology is not quite so sharp. Many of the arguments we will examine may look like attempts to establish religious belief on rational principles, but actually turn out to have their origin in attempts to provide rational explanations within religious belief systems. None the less, our concern here will be with the philosophy of religion as contrasted with theology. It will start not from the assumption that any religious beliefs are true, but with an open-minded approach to arguments for and against religion.

Many of the arguments that will be considered appear in different forms in different classic texts. For example, the ontological argument for the existence of God has been put forward in different forms by both St Anselm and René Descartes. Because of the brevity of this book, I will not be presenting versions of such arguments specific to individual texts. My aim is rather to examine the general forms of such arguments and the general objections which can be raised against them. That way we can identify the issues which cut across many different versions of the arguments without getting bogged down in details specific to one or two writers.

There is another issue which concerns the pronoun used for God. God is usually referred to as 'he' (or 'He'). For even the most literal-minded of religious believers, there is something odd about this. After all, God is supposed to be neither human nor material. In any case, the whole category of maleness only has sense in the context of biological creatures which sexually reproduce, and whatever God is, it isn't such an animal. Therefore, the idea that God is male is somewhat baffling. It would be equally absurd to rectify this by supposing God to be female and to use the pronoun 'she'. My solution here is to call God 'it'. While this is unsatisfactory to the extent that the English 'it' refers to objects rather than beings and that if God does exist, then it is a being rather than an object, it seems to me to be the least bad option available.

A final point to bear in mind is that the agenda of the philosophy of religion as studied in the English-speaking world is largely set by issues arising out of the Judaeo-Christian tradition. This is, of course, a limitation, since if our starting point were some of the eastern religions, for example, different philosophical questions would arise. In following this agenda, then, I am following what the syllabuses of many philosophy of religion courses dictate.

▶ What is God?

Much of what we will be discussing in this chapter concerns the existence or non-existence of God. But what do we mean by God? In the Judaeo-Christian tradition, God is usually characterised by what we can call the three omnis, 'omni' being a prefix meaning 'all'.

First, God is taken to be omnipotent or all-powerful. That means that God can do anything. If God wants to destroy everything in an instant, or create infinite matter out of nothing, then it can do so. But could God create an open door that is shut, or a square circle? Could God make one and one equal 3? This seems absurd and many theologians have been happy to accept that God cannot do things which are logically impossible such as these. In this way, we can see that things like square circles are just nonsenses, and to say that God cannot create them is not to place limits on its power.

Second, God is taken to be omnibenevolent or all-loving. In the words of the famous hymn, 'God is love'. Therefore, there is no limit to God's caring. God would not allow anyone to suffer because it had run out of love. This is important for the question of why there is suffering in the world, as we shall see in the next section.

Third, God is taken to be omniscient or all-knowing. No-one can hide from God because God can see everything and knows everything, including your most intimate, private thoughts. God is the ultimate Big Brother.

In addition to these three characteristics, some add that God is omnipresent or everywhere. This is actually a matter of dispute. While some theologians understand God to be at all places at all times (or 'immanent' in creation), others see God as existing somehow 'outside' of its creation (or transcendent). Because of this disagreement, the idea that God is omnipresent is not part of the core of the Judaeo-Christian conception of God.

Some people are concerned by the fact that God is supposed to be omniscient because it seems to present a problem for human free will. For example, if God knows that I am about to choose coffee rather than tea, does that mean my choice was not really free, that it was somehow predetermined and beyond my control?

This worry is based on a misunderstanding. The fact that God knows what will happen next does not necessarily mean that the future is fixed. If God is transcendent and exists outside of space and time, for example, then the fact that it can see the future does not mean the future is not the result of our free choices. God could know what we will do freely without that in any way compromising out freedom. Even if God is immanent in time and space, the mere ability to see the future does not mean the future is fixed. There may be other reasons to suppose we don't have free will, but God's knowledge of the future is not one of them.

A far more serious problem for the conception of God sketched out concerns the question of why there is evil and suffering in the world. This is the so-called problem of evil.

▶ The problem of evil

The problem of evil is misleadingly named because it is not just the problem of evil in the sense of the wicked things people do. It is really a problem of 'bad things'. These bad things can be classified into two types. First, there is moral evil, which are bad things that are the result of human action, such as torture and cruelty. The second type is natural evil, which are bad things that just happen, such as floods, disease, earthquakes and accidents.

The problem for the traditional conception of God is that there is a lot of both kinds of evil about. In fact, there is so much that it leads many to ask how the existence of such suffering is compatible with the existence of God as traditionally conceived.

The problem can be stated starkly. We know that there is evil (in the senses defined) in the world. If God exists, then how can we explain this evil? There seem to be three possible explanations. It could be that God doesn't know about it, but that would mean God isn't omniscient. It could be that God doesn't care about it, but that would mean God isn't omnibenevolent. It could be that God can't stop it, but that would mean God isn't omnipotent. So it seems that the only way to reconcile the existence of evil with the existence of God is to radically change our idea of what God is: God cannot be omniscient, omnibenevolent and omnipotent.

Some people claim that this is enough to show that God doesn't exist, at least not the God many people worship and believe in. But is there a way out? Is there an explanation of how God could know about suffering, care about suffering, be able to do something about that suffering, yet still allow it to go on?

Attempts to offer such explanations are known as theodicies and they come in many forms.

Some theodicies are extremely implausible. For instance, some deny the premise that there is actually any evil in the world at all. Things may look bad from where we're standing, but that's just because we can't see the whole picture. From where God's sitting, everything looks fine. It is hard to see how anyone could seriously believe this, at least while keeping their humanity intact. To look at the horrors of Auschwitz, for example, and say that it only looks bad because we can't see the whole picture seems to be callous at the very least.

More plausible theodicies do not deny the reality of evil, but attempt to show that, in the long run, it is better they exist than that they don't. Just as a dentist asks you to put up with some pain because you'll benefit in the long run, so, on this view, God allows us to suffer because it is necessary in the long run. This doesn't deny the reality of suffering, but it explains why it is necessary.

But what could possibly make all the suffering in the world worthwhile? One surprisingly popular answer is the so-called free will defence. I say surprisingly popular because it seems so obviously inadequate. The free will defence argues that God had two choices: it either created creatures with free will and the opportunity to freely choose good and thus enjoy eternal life; or it didn't create such creatures. The universe is a better place if such creatures exist. So God created them. But if such creatures exist, then they are bound to choose bad as well as good, causing suffering. So evil is bound to exist, but this is a price worth paying.

As it stands, this defence is hopeless because it only covers moral evil, not natural evil. It still doesn't explain disease, earthquakes and so on. So the free will defence has to be modified to say that such things are necessary in order that we can learn from them and grow spiritually. In other, words, it is only by confronting suffering that we come to be able to choose good.

Even in its modified form the defence is weak. The necessity of confronting suffering seems rather implausible. Some people suffer much more than others. Does that mean they are better people as a result? Do only they get to heaven? This leads into the general difficulty that the scale of the suffering seems disproportionate. Why do some people die slowly, in agonising pain, sometimes with no-one there to witness it and so learn from it?

It is also extremely dubious to suppose that this terrible suffering is really necessary. People can learn in different ways. For some people, it is enough to see that something is harmful for them to avoid it, whereas others have to actually experience the bad consequences before they shun it. This shows that there is nothing fixed and necessary about the way we learn. God could have made us better or worse learners by nature. God seems to be some kind of sadist if it has designed us in such a way that we can only learn through such terrible means.

In short, the free will defence fails to explain the variations in suffering we endure and the extremes which some people have to put up with. It also seems to be based on a cruel doctrine that we need to be made to suffer in order to learn. If the universe is this cruel, then surely that gives us more reason to doubt that it is under the control of a good God.

This leads to a different kind of way of putting the problem of evil. Let us accept that there is some rational way of reconciling God's existence with the existence of evil. If this could be done and God did exist, where would that leave us? For many, it seems we are left with the shocking truth that God is prepared to allow terrible suffering as a means to an end. We may feel that there are cruelties which God has allowed which could never be justified as a means to an end. If God allows these things, then that means God is not worthy of our worship. Put this way, the problem of evil shows that either God does not exist or that God is morally repugnant.

▶ Faith and reason

Many believers find this style of arguing unsatisfactory. There seems to be something wrong about expecting God's ways to somehow be comprehensible to us. Shouldn't we just allow that God's purposes may be mysterious and that we cannot expect to fully understand them? We may not be able to see what could possibly make suffering worthwhile, but we can't see what choices God had, or how wonderful the rewards of life after death are. Can't we just trust that, after death, we will all come to see that God's purposes are indeed good?

This objection runs up against the problem of distinguishing the philosophy of religion from theology. In theology, it may be enough to say that we can understand so much but beyond that, all is mystery. If we are starting from a faith in God's goodness, then we can try and explain the existence of evil as best we can, but accept that our explanation may be incomplete. But the philosophy of religion does not start by presuming faith. If we cannot solve the problem of evil rationally, then our conclusion should be that it is not rational to believe in or worship God.

This, however, does invite a further, vital question. Though it may not be rational to worship or believe in God, doesn't faith go beyond what is rational? Must we be constrained by what is rational when it comes to religious belief?

There are many ways of considering this question, but if we are working within the philosophy of religion, the way to do this is to consider from a rational point of view what the limits of rationality might be and how faith can or can't go beyond reason. If we just say that faith has its reasons of which reason knows nothing, we have effectively given up on approaching issues of religion philosophically.

The idea that reason has its limits has a long pedigree in philosophy. Kant once said that his philosophy placed limits on reason so as to make room for faith. He attempted to show that there were some questions about which reason must remain silent, but which are still vital to human life. In these areas, it is legitimate to make one's decisions on the basis of faith.

A similar line of reasoning was followed by William James (1842–1910), who argued that there are many issues where it is acceptable to make decisions of belief on non-rational grounds, and God's existence is one of them.

James's argument rests on the idea that we sometimes have a choice between two or more competing hypotheses, but we lack evidential or rational grounds for making the choice. (For the sake of simplicity I shall continue to talk of instances where there are just two options.) Of course, what we might do in such a situation is simply not make a choice. We can just suspend judgement and say we don't know which hypothesis is true. But in what James calls genuine options, we cannot do this. We have to make a choice and, in the absence of rational grounds for making that choice, we have to let our feelings – or our 'passional nature' – guide us.

These genuine options have three characteristics. First, the hypothesis in question must be a 'live' option. A live option is a hypothesis which is a serious possibility. If I were to ask you to consider the hypothesis that the moon is a lump of cheese, that would not be a live option. It is simply not a serious possibility. But the hypothesis that the mafia had JFK killed is a live hypothesis. You may not believe it, but it is a serious possibility. God's existence is, according to James, also a live hypothesis. Whether we believe in God or not, its existence is a serious possibility.

The second key feature of a genuine option is that it is forced. A forced option is one where you have two choices and there is no middle ground. For example, if I ask you if you want tea with or without sugar, that is not a forced option because you could choose not to have tea at all. But if I ask you to accept something I say as true, you either do or you do not. If you say, 'I'm not sure, I suspend judgement', then you have effectively refused to accept what I say. Belief in God is, for James, a forced option, because we either believe in God or we withhold our belief, by believing God doesn't exist or by suspending judgement. Either way, we have chosen not to believe.

The last feature of a genuine option is that it is in some way momentous. Watching a soap opera is both a live and forced option. It is a real possibility and I either watch it or I don't. But it is not momentous. My life is not significantly changed depending on my decision. Belief in God, however, is momentous. It makes a great deal of difference to our lives (and possibly our afterlives) whether we believe in God or not. It affects the whole way in which we view the world.

So, for James, belief in God is a genuine option because it is live, forced and momentous. But neither reason nor evidence can decide whether we should believe in God or not. Therefore, we are entitled – or even obliged – to allow our feelings to guide us. If we decide to believe in God, therefore, we act on a faith which goes beyond reason, but only because our decision must be made beyond reason's domain.

James's argument is a very interesting and sophisticated one, but it does have many weaknesses. First, many atheists do not think that God's existence is a live option. Their reflections lead them to believe that the very idea of a God in the Judaeo-Christian mould is ridiculous. For such people, God's existence is as dead an option as the moon being made of cheese.

Second, we might resist James's definition of a forced option. On James's account, it seems that suspending judgement is never permitted, because to suspend judgement is to withhold assent and this is classified as rejecting a belief. But surely there is a difference between rejecting a hypothesis and suspending judgement about it. This difference is deemed unimportant by James.

Third, we could disagree that reason and evidence don't settle the question for us. It may well be the case that one cannot prove whether God does or doesn't exist. But the balance of evidence and arguments may tilt much more one way than the other. If this is so, then we don't need to rely purely on our passional nature. Our brains could still have the most important role to play.

James's argument aims to justify making a decision of faith without the support of reason by showing that by the standards of reason itself, such decisions are justified. It is certainly a clever argument, but whether it succeeds is a matter for debate.

▶ Betting on God

Blaise Pascal offered a very different kind of argument which attempted to justify belief in God in the absence of proof or conclusive evidence. His argument is known as 'Pascal's Wager' because it attempts to show that belief in God is like a bet you would be foolish not to make.

The essence of the argument is that we have two possibilities: God does or doesn't exist. We don't have proof either way, so you've got to choose which one to believe. If you choose to believe in God and worship it, two things could happen. If God exists, you've chosen the right answer and heaven awaits (along with some rewards in this life to do with tranquillity of mind and so on). If God doesn't exist, you still get the rewards in this life. Your piety would have come at a small cost of course, but since death is the end, nothing much matters anyway.

If you choose not to believe in God, there are likewise two possibilities. If God doesn't exist, you were right, but death is the end and it's all meaningless anyway. You win, but your victory is hollow. If God does exist, your disbelief means you risk hellfire and damnation, or at the very least miss out on fast-track access through the pearly gates.

So which is the better bet? It would seem that belief in God is. Only this one gives you a chance of eternal life and it comes at little cost. The other choices have few potential rewards and carry great risks. So belief in God is the best bet.

The argument is clever, but it is sometimes hard to see why it has commanded so much attention. The first problem is, if I believe in God, which God do I believe in? If I choose the wrong religion or sect, I also risk hellfire and damnation. More serious still is the question of why a great God would accept into heaven people who choose to believe in it on the basis that it's a good bet instead of others who don't, but who live good lives. Pascal acknowledges that belief must be sincere but he argues that, once you accept the bet, if you just practice living a religious life you will come to believe sincerely. But this seems to be a double-bluff: you first trick yourself into believing sincerely, and then God will accept this sincerity and let you into heaven.

Both these problems touch on the wider issue that, for the non-believer, the whole idea that God decides how to reward people on the basis of what they believe about it is crazy. Is God some kind of insecure egomaniac who treats people better or worse depending on how much they worship it? The atheist finds something strange in the mindset of religious believers who think that decisions about eternal life and damnation are made on this basis. To put it in terms of another bet, the atheist might think that if there is a God, it is much more likely that it decides what happens after life on the basis of how a person has lived than on whether they join the right religion.

▶ The status of religious language

Just as many religious believers think there is something inappropriate about trying to understand religion in purely rational terms, many others think that it is inappropriate to try to understand religious language in ordinary terms. When, for example, a Christian priest takes the bread and wine in a communion service and says, 'This is the body and blood of Jesus Christ', it would be crass to take these words in their everyday senses. Normally, if we say something is the body and blood of someone, that means, if we were to analyse it, we would find it was composed of flesh and blood. Hardly anyone thinks this is what would happen were you to analyse the communion bread and wine. Whatever it means to say the bread and wine is flesh and blood, it isn't that.

However, it is difficult to move on from this to find a way of understanding religious language that is satisfactory. For a start, most religious believers would not want to say that the language they use is simply metaphorical or figurative.

To understand how Jesus is the son of God, for instance, we may have to understand 'son' differently from normal, but Christians surely don't mean that Jesus isn't really God's son and that the phrase 'son of God' is just a metaphor. Of course, religious texts may include metaphors, but if all religious language were understood this way, believing in a religion would not require belief in anything literally true, but merely the admiration of a kind of body of poetry.

So the dilemma facing religious believers is this. If religious language is interpreted as normal language, much in religious creeds just seems to be absurd or demonstrably false. Jesus can't literally be all God and all man. He can't literally be the son of God. The communion bread and wine can't literally be the body and blood of Christ. But if religious language is taken to be figurative or metaphorical, religious beliefs lose their substance. For instance, belief in life after death does not add up to much if this is just a belief in a metaphorical life after death. An atheist can believe in that kind of immortality. And if 'son of God' is a metaphor, what makes Jesus so special? Aren't we all, metaphorically speaking, sons and daughters of God? But if religious language is neither literally nor metaphorically true, what kind of status does it have? And doesn't the whole attempt to make an exception for religious language look like a desperate measure to preserve truth and meaning in a body of belief that is just out of kilter with the rest of our knowledge and beliefs?

In the twentieth century, some have seen a solution to this problem in the later philosophy of Ludwig Wittgenstein (1889–1951). The way in which Wittgenstein understood language seems to make room for different types of language to have different rules, without needing to make a special case for religion. Wittgenstein rejected the model of language which saw words and sentences as mapping directly on to the world, rather like the way captions map on to the pictures they are placed under. For example, it is common to think that a sentence like 'the cat sat on the mat' means what is does, and is true or false, because of the relations the words in the sentence have to objects in the real world – the cat and the mat. On this model, meaning and truth in language is just a matter of words and sentences corresponding to things in the world.

The problem is that if you look at what rules govern this correspondence, things begin to look much more difficult. For instance, what if I say, 'Jenny is playing a game'? What rule determines whether these words correspond to reality? You might think the answer is simple: the words correspond if there is a person called Jenny and she is playing a game. But the hard question is this: what rule tells me if Jenny is playing a game? What are the rules that tell me when a word like 'game' is being applied correctly? Attempting to answer this question can be frustrating, because in one sense we all know full well what playing a game involves. But if you try and articulate that in a clear set of rules, you will almost certainly fail. There are just too many ways in which one can play a game.

Further, the same activity, such as a fight, can start as not a game and become a game, or the other way around. The word has too fluid and flexible a meaning to be captured in a finite set of rules.

Wittgenstein's point here is that using a word correctly is not about learning a set of rules so that we can label items in the world correctly. It is much more like learning a skill. We understand what a word means when we can use it correctly. Compare this to learning how to use something like a baseball bat. We know someone has learned how to use a baseball bat, not when they can tell us all about bats, but when they can go out into the field and whack the ball well. In the same way, learning to use language is about using words appropriately and in the right context. This is captured in Wittgenstein's advice that to understand a word, you shouldn't ask for the meaning, you should ask for the use.

How does this relate to religious language? Wittgenstein's theory is seen by some as a rebuttal of those who demand of religious language that it operates in ordinary or scientifically explicable terms. If you ask to examine the communion wine to see if it is blood, for instance, you are making the mistake of assuming that there is a clear rule which governs the use of the word 'blood' and that this rule is basically a scientific one. However, for the religious believer, there are other uses of this word. 'Blood' has a sacred significance and a use in the communion service which can't be simply explained in terms of mere metaphor or science. The only way to really understand this use is to live within the religious community and use the word for yourself. Just as you can only learn how to use the baseball bat by practising in the park, so you can only learn how to use language by practising it in the community in which it is used. So to understand religious language, you need to see how it is used in the religious community.

Wittgenstein's theory is extremely subtle and rich and merits a close reading. Its main danger is that it can be used as a justification for obscurantism – the covering up of vague or confused ideas in a veil of impenetratable language. After all, couldn't anyone, if their beliefs are under attack, turn around and say, 'You just don't understand how these words are used in our language community'?

In addition to this, Wittgenstein's views may also lead to relativism, where there are no common standards to decide between competing claims to truth and where every community has its own truths. This is a consequence many Wittgensteinians are prepared to accept, but it troubles many others who believe truth and falsehood depend not on what we say and think, but on how things are.

▶ The ontological argument

The issues we have looked at so far, surrounding the concept of God, the nature of evil, religious language and the relation between faith and reason, are perhaps the most interesting in the philosophy of religion. But when the subject is taught, these issues are often considered second, not first. Priority in the syllabuses tends to go to a series of largely medieval arguments for the existence of God. These arguments are certainly of interest, as we shall see. But in many ways it is odd they still command so much attention, for they are among the weakest arguments in the history of philosophy.

One of the most interesting and difficult of these is the ontological argument for the existence of God, which appears in its most famous guises in the writings of St Anselm and Descartes. As with many of these arguments, there is no one single 'Ontological Argument'. Rather, there are a number of different arguments, all of which share a basic common form. Ontological arguments attempt to show that God must exist as a matter of necessity and that we can know this simply by considering what the concept of God means.

In its simplest form, the argument attempts to show that it is a contradiction to say that God does not exist. Consider as an example what we can and cannot say about triangles. Without making any presumptions about whether triangles actually exist or not, we know by considering what it means for something to be a triangle that triangles must have three sides and that a four-sided triangle is a contradiction in terms. Now consider the concept of God. God is, as we have seen, all the omnis – omnipotent, omniscient and omnibenevolent. But surely something which has all these features must also exist. You can't be all-powerful if you don't actually exist. So it seems existence is built into the concept of God. So just as a four-sided triangle is a contradiction in terms, so is a non-existent God. Therefore, God must exist.

Although this is a simplified version of the argument, it does contain the essence of all ontological arguments, as can be seen by looking at a more sophisticated formulation. One seemingly unobjectionable definition of God is 'the greatest being imaginable'. Let us now suppose that such a being does not exist. Now, though, it seems that I can imagine a being greater than this, namely, the greatest being imaginable which actually exists. But, of course, if such a being can be imagined, then our original, non-existent God is not the greatest being imaginable after all. The only way to get out of this contradiction is to suppose that such a being does exist. That is the only way the concept of the greatest being imaginable makes sense and doesn't contradict itself.

As is clear, although the formulation of this argument is a little more sophisticated, in essence the same point is being made. God's existence is deemed to be necessary because the concept of a non-existent God is taken to be in some way incoherent or self-contradictory.

The problem with this argument is evident as soon as we apply the same logic to something else, like the greatest athlete imaginable. If the greatest athlete imaginable doesn't exist, then it seems we could imagine an athlete greater than this, namely the greatest athlete imaginable who does actually exist. This would make the non-existent greatest athlete imaginable not the greatest athlete imaginable after all. So it seems the greatest athlete imaginable must exist.

As should be clear, the same argument could apply to the greatest pizza imaginable, or the greatest symphony imaginable. Worse, it could also apply to non-existent entities. What about the greatest dragon or phoenix imaginable? Or the greatest half-man, half-cheeseburger imaginable? All these things must exist if the logic of the ontological argument is right.

Of course, there have been attempts to show that God is a special case, and that the logic of the ontological argument can't be extended to just anything. But most philosophers do accept the logic of the argument is flawed. So where does the mistake lie exactly? The problem seems to be that the argument makes a leap between concepts and actual existence. But there is no direct link between the two. For example, in the case of triangles, the fact that a triangle must have three sides does not mean that any actual triangles exist. It does mean that if a triangle exists, then it must have three sides, but this is still an 'if'. From what must be true about the concept of a triangle, therefore, nothing about the actual existence or not of triangles can be inferred.

Similarly, if we consider the concept of God, we might conclude that if God exists, God is the most perfect being imaginable. But this is still an if. We cannot conclude that God must exist because the concept of God is the concept of a supremely perfect being. Considerations of the concept of God can never tell us whether there is an actual being in the universe to which the concept applies.

The ontological argument is therefore considered by most philosophers to have failed. But there are other arguments for God's existence which we also have to consider.

▶ The cosmological argument

The ontological argument has a fishy smell about it and is intuitively unpersuasive, but it is difficult to pinpoint exactly what is wrong with it. The cosmological argument, on the other hand, is one of the most intuitively plausible arguments for the existence of God, but its faults are all too glaring.

The cosmological argument is really little more than the argument that everything must have a cause and therefore the universe itself must have a cause. Since that cause cannot be the universe itself, it must be something else, something powerful enough to bring everything into existence. God is the best candidate for this, since only God seems powerful enough to be this cause.

One important feature to note about this argument is that, unlike the ontological argument, it is based on the evidence of experience rather than watertight logic. In philosophical terms, it is an *a posteriori* argument, not an *a priori* one. This means that we should not expect the conclusion to follow as a matter of necessity from the premises. It is enough that the conclusion is the best way of explaining the evidence.

The problem with the argument is that there is no justification for virtually every part of it. Even the basic premise that everything has a cause is debatable. It is not out of logical necessity that we say everything must have a cause. The idea of an uncaused event is not a logical contradiction in the way that a square circle is. Rather, we say everything must have a cause because this is what experience teaches us. But experience only teaches us about events in the universe as it actually exists. Experience is silent about what happened before the universe existed, or at the point where it came into existence. So although experience does teach us that every event *in* the universe has a cause, it does not and cannot tell us that the universe as a whole must have a cause.

Nevertheless, some might say that if there are two hypotheses – that the universe has a cause or it doesn't – the hypothesis that it does is more plausible. This response faces two problems. First, this plausibility seems to be based on the assumption that everything has a cause, which, as we have seen, has no foundation in logic or experience. Second, if we say that God is the cause, we are saying that there is at least one thing in the universe which does not have a cause – God. So we are contradicting our major premise that everything must have a cause. Third, even if we accept that the universe has an uncaused cause, the jump from this to God is extremely large. All we need to end the causal chain is the idea of an uncaused first cause. Why should we attribute to this all the characteristics of God?

The cosmological argument seems, then, to boil down to this: there must be at least one uncaused cause in the universe and that God is the best candidate for this. Although the first part of this proposition seems reasonable (though not beyond dispute), it is the second part which is really speculative. In essence, the argument seems to be that we have no idea what kind of thing this uncaused cause could be so we'll say it's God. This is a very weak form of argument. Historically, God has always been invoked to explain the mysterious or unexplained. When people didn't know where thunder came from, they attributed it to God. When they didn't understand meteorology, they thought God was pulling the weather levers. Such a 'God of the gaps' is very vulnerable to advances in knowledge. As soon as we understand how a part of nature works, another role for God goes. Now God has been demoted to the first cause, the last part of nature where it is felt we need to invoke God to explain things. But this is a dangerous place for God to be, for modern physics is even grappling with the question of how the universe began and is coming up with explanations which do not need God. An argument for the existence of God which is based on needing God to explain the unexplained would therefore seem to be a very weak, vulnerable and discredited form of argument.

▶ The teleological argument

If the cosmological argument deserves short-shrift then so too does the teleological argument. It too is intuitively appealing and is based on experience, but even more than the cosmological argument, it has been made to look hopelessly naïve by scientific advances.

The teleological argument starts with the observation that the universe is intricate and orderly. As one of the original proponents of the argument, William Paley, noted, when we find something like a watch, inspect it and find all its parts are working harmoniously and in an orderly fashion, we reason that someone must have designed and made the watch. We do not think that such objects just spring into existence or grow on trees. But if we reason thus when we look at something so simple as a pocket watch, surely when we see something so vast and intricate as the universe, it is reasonable to suppose that an intelligent designer and maker created it. The only thing we can conceive of which comes close to the description of such a creator is God, for only something all-powerful and all-knowing would have the intellect and resources to design such a universe.

The argument has two main weaknesses. First, the analogy between the watch and the universe is very weak. We know that artefacts such as watches have makers because we have experience of watches and watchmakers and we know that you can't have the former without the latter. But this is not the case with nature. We do not find a beautiful wilderness and assume it must be the work of a landscape gardener. It is only when a landscape has been clearly ordered in a particular way, typical of the work of humans, that we believe a gardener is responsible. What this example shows is that the hallmarks of intelligent design are only found in certain kinds of things. Wildernesses, animals and natural phenomena do not bear the hallmarks of intelligent design in the same way as watches, cars and buildings do.

Further, we have no experience at all as to what the ultimate causes of things in nature are. As far as we do have experience of the causes of natural phenomena, these are definitely not intelligent designers. Mountain ranges are caused by shifts in the Earth's plates, storms by falling air pressure, cliffs by gradual erosion of the coastline. In so far as experience tells us anything at all about the causes of things in nature, it tells us they are not the product of intelligent design.

But surely, it might be argued, the best explanation for the overall order of the universe is that there is an intelligent designer? The analogy with artefacts may not work, but none the less, we know that had just a few things been slightly different at the start of the universe with the Big Bang, none of this would be here at all. Surely something intelligent must be behind it?

The idea that God is the best explanation for the order we find in the universe leads to the second main objection to the teleological argument. The problem is simply that God is not the best explanation at all. To say God created the order of the universe is to say we don't know how the order in the universe came about, we just think God is responsible for it. This isn't an explanation. It would be like saying that you can explain how a murder was carried out simply by identifying someone as the murderer. But what is worse, science can explain a lot of the order in the universe without the need to invoke God. Most power-fully, evolutionary theory turns the idea of intelligent design on its head.

It is worth spending a little time looking at evolution because it is often mis-understood. Consider something like the human ear. Pre-Darwin, it would seem natural to think that something as useful as the ear must have been the product of some kind of design. God gave us ears to hear – how else could we have got them? Evolutionary theory explains how we got ears without the need for the intervention of a benign, intelligent designer. This is, crudely, how it works.

When an animal or plant reproduces, it never reproduces itself exactly. Rather like a photocopier, or a game of Chinese whispers, small changes or 'mutations' occur from generation to generation. Some of these random mutations will bene-fit the offspring and some will not. So, for example, an early ancestor of *homo sapiens* reproduces and one of its children has a minute sensitivity to sound whereas another does not. This sensitivity gives that animal an advantage over its peers, since it provides an early warning system for approaching danger, for example. So that particular animal is more likely to reproduce and pass on this sensitivity to its own offspring. These will, in turn, have an advantage over their peers. So, over time, the proportion of these animals which have this sensitivity to sound increases. Further, those which have a greater sensitivity to sound will stand more chance of survival than those who have a lesser sensitivity. So a pro-cess begins by which, generation to generation, without intelligent design or purpose, those with a greater sensitivity to sound tend to survive more than those with a lesser sensitivity. And so, over time, this sensitivity develops until many millions of years later, we have the human ear.

Many creationists will say that evolutionary theory is incomplete and con-tested. In fact, it is one of the most tested and proven theories in science. It can be hard to fully conceive because it works over vast time-scales. It is virtually impossible to really imagine an ear developing over millions of years from a small mutation which first gave an animal a minute sensitivity to sound. But the failure here is purely one of imagination. One can understand how the process works and even observe the process at work in experiments on fruit flies, for example, which breed quickly enough for scientists to actually witness evolution at work.

Evolution shows how you can end up with order in the universe, even organs which appear to be designed to fulfil a function, such as hearing, without the need for an intelligent designer. Other branches of science, such as physics, explain the order in parts of the universe other than human life. In the light of this, it is hard to see how the hypothesis of an intelligent designer is the best explanation for the order of the universe.

▶ Religious experience

The apparent failure of the traditional arguments for the existence of God doesn't bother most religious believers. One reason for this is that belief in God is very rarely founded on such arguments. People do not read about the cosmological argument and go off and get baptised the next day. What does tend to ground religious belief is personal experience. The physicist Russell Stannard, echoing Jung, captured this when he said in an interview: 'I don't have to believe in God, I know that God exists – that is how I feel.' At the end of the day, all we have considered so far in this chapter is irrelevant to many with faith. What counts for them is the inner conviction that God exists, often based on a feeling that they have had some direct experience of God's existence.

These experiences may take many forms. They may be visions of saints or prophets. They may be no more than inner convictions. They may be a sense of God in nature. Rather than look at each type of experience individually, I will just talk about religious experience as one kind of thing which is characterised by any kind of personal conviction that God exists based on one's own private experience. (Public experience of miracles is discussed in the next section.)

The philosopher Alvin Plantinga has argued that it is quite right to take the evidence of such experiences as basic beliefs, beliefs which form the foundations for our other beliefs, but which themselves do not need to be justified by other beliefs. Just as we do not need to justify the belief that we exist and have experiences of objects and other people, so our experience of God's presence (if we have it) stands as basic and without need of justification.

It is easy to see why, for those who have such convictions, no further justification seems required. But there are several reasons for not just accepting the evidence of personal experience in this case.

First, religious beliefs are very different from beliefs in things such as our own existence and our experience of objects. It is true that in both cases we cannot easily doubt that the experience is real. We cannot doubt that we seem to exist, we cannot doubt that objects seem to exist and the religious believer may not be able to doubt that God seems to exist. In each case, what is undoubtedly real is the experience. What can be doubted in each case is whether the experience corresponds to an independent reality. The arguments concerning the real existence of the self and the material world are many and complicated. But virtually everyone would agree that, even if we cannot adequately justify our conviction that we and the external world exist, we cannot dispense with the conviction that they do. We can, however, easily dispense with the conviction that God exists. In a recent survey, more than half the British population said that they didn't believe in God. The question wasn't asked, but it is clear that very few, if any, would have said they didn't believe in themselves or the external world. What this illustrates is that beliefs based on religious experiences are dispensable in a way in which basic beliefs about self and world are not. So they are not basic beliefs in quite the same way.

Further, the beliefs which religious experiences claim to justify are disputable in a way in which other basic beliefs are not. For example, if you're sitting next to someone and they point and say 'there's a pink elephant' and you see it too, that is a reason to think the pink elephant is there. But if you can't see the elephant, the suspicion is that the other person is hallucinating or is making it up. Religious experiences are more like the latter experiences than the former. Someone can claim to be in the presence of God while the person next to them feels no such thing. That is to say, the belief created by the experience is not subject to independent confirmation in the way in which other basic experiences are. This is usually the hallmark of an experience which is not of something real.

The important thing to note here is that such experiences may be utterly convincing to the person having them. But we do not take the vividness of the experience to be evidence that the thing the experience is of really exists. We just accept that people's experiences can mislead them. In the same way, the non-believer will say that the conviction the believer has is no evidence that God actually exists and that they too should accept this.

But why should the religious believer doubt their own experiences? After all, it is not quite like the pink elephant. What they claim to experience isn't visible, for instance, so one might expect others not to be aware of it. And many religious believers share the same convictions. So there is some support from the experience of others.

The response to this is that religious experiences contradict one another. If religious experience were a reliable source of belief, then we would not find these contradictions. For instance, people use religious experiences to justify their beliefs in a variety of different Gods. People use it to justify a variety of different, conflicting actions. Some will say they felt God telling them not to work on the Sabbath, whereas others will say they felt God telling them to do the opposite. We should also remember that many criminals have reported that they were told what to do by God. The notorious 'Yorkshire Ripper', Peter Sutcliffe, sexually assaulted and killed several women because he heard God telling him to do so.

The point is that if religious experience were a reliable basis for belief, we would find that religious experiences produced the same beliefs time and time again. But what in fact seems to happen is that people have religious experiences and they interpret them or take them to justify whatever religious beliefs they already have or are dominant in their cultures. In this way, it seems that religious experiences are not a reliable foundation for religious belief.

To someone who has a religious belief, their own experience of what they take to be God often does seem to be enough to convince them of the veracity of their beliefs. The problem is that the question of whether something is true or false is separate from the question of how firmly one is convinced that it is true or false. One cannot use the firmness of one's convictions as evidence for the truth of that of which one is convinced.

▶ Miracles

There is one kind of religious experience which is not private but, at least in theory, public. Miracles have been reported in the literatures of all the great religions of the world. Do these miracles provide any evidence that God does indeed exist?

To many it seems bizarre that such a question can still be asked in any seriousness. After all, we only seem to get reports of supposed miracles in ancient texts which are not known for their historical accuracy, or in far-flung corners of the world where superstition still rules the day. Can it be a coincidence that miracles don't happen in Times Square or Piccadilly Circus, but only places where their veracity cannot be checked?

Such is the rarity of anything that even looks like being a genuine miracle that it became headline news for several days when a statue of an elephant in a Hindu temple in North London seemed to start absorbing milk offered up to it from spoons. The fact that it was made of a porous stone and that much of the milk ended up on the floor below it did not stop people being amazed by the statue's 'drinking'.

The Roman Catholic Church also continues to record miracle healings at Lourdes. This is very odd since it is a fact that some people do get better for no apparent reason, especially if their mental attitude is positive. This suggests that if thousands of sick people passed through any spot in the world, believing it would help them, some would get better without any obvious reason. But at Lourdes, such a recovery is called a miracle.

The point is that there is no good evidence at all that miracles take or have taken place. Therefore, the idea that philosophers should consider whether miracles would provide evidence for the existence of God seems as crazy as asking them to consider whether sightings of fairies would provide evidence for the existence of goblins.

None the less, the question is asked and we therefore need to consider whether miracles would, if they occurred, provide any evidence for the existence of God. To answer this we need to consider what a miracle is. Many follow Hume in defining a miracle as a violation of the laws of nature. Some disagree with this and say that a miracle can be merely an extraordinary event or even an ordinary event with religious significance. But this seems to be stretching the definition of the word. A miracle is only a miracle if the ordinary course of events has been altered. Otherwise, what happens is merely a coincidence or good luck. And if the normal course of events has been altered, a law of nature has to be breeched. So Hume's definition does seem to be right.

Hume went on to argue that we can never have any good reason to suppose such miracles can occur. This is because all of experience confirms to us that natural laws are never breeched. Therefore, whenever one seems to be breeched, it is always more reasonable to assume that we have been tricked, or that there is another kind of unseen, natural cause in operation, or that what we thought was a law of nature is not, in fact, so.

For example, let's say you see a good illusionist, such as David Copperfield, make a huge truck seemingly disappear. That would seem to be a miracle. But you would be very gullible if you thought that Copperfield had actually broken the laws of nature. You would assume one of the three things set out above. One possibility is that this is a trick and he hasn't made the truck disappear at all. Another possibility is that he has made it disappear, but by some unseen cause, such as a hidden trap door. The third, most outlandish, possibility is that Copperfield has discovered a new law of nature which explains how objects can be made to disappear into thin air. The one thing you wouldn't think was that he had performed a miracle.

If this is what you would think when you saw someone make a truck vanish in front on your very eyes, why should you think anything different for other alleged miracles? It seems bizarre that we can see someone perform a very impressive trick, such as seeming to cut a person into two, and accept that it is just an illusion, but we can also see something relatively unimpressive, like a statue absorbing milk, and think this is a miracle. Hume's argument is that experience teaches us that we always have more reason to suppose that natural laws have not been breeched than that they have. It is just gullible to think anything else.

We might question Hume's principle and wonder if nothing at all would ever count as evidence for a miracle. But since even the greatest of reported miracles that can be taken to bear any relation to what actually happened are not earth-shatteringly impressive, it is not clear why we should worry about such outlandish possibilities. Miracles do not provide any evidence for God's existence, then, because there is no good reason to suppose miracles occur.

▶ God and morality

One reason why people think it is important that God exists is that without God, it might seem that morality is impossible. The existence of moral law implies the existence of a moral lawgiver. The only being in a position to issue such laws is God, so if God doesn't exist, then morality is not possible.

Some have even used this as an argument for God's existence. Given that there is such a thing as morality, and given that only God can be the source of it, God must exist. This argument's first premise is questionable, since the fact that we do follow moral rules and believe there is a morality is no guarantee that morality exists independently of us. It could just be that when we think we are following real moral laws, we are merely following human conventions or laws established by us rather than God. So although it is unquestionably true that morality exists in some form, it is not obvious that this is morality in the sense of a set of laws laid down by divine authority.

The second premise of the argument is more interesting, for whether or not the argument from morality's existence to God's existence works, there is still an issue of whether or not the very possibility of morality somehow depends on God.

In fact, a very persuasive argument that morality does not depend on God was put forward over 2000 years ago by Plato, in a dialogue called *Euthypryo*. The argument is very simple and is based on the possible answers to a simple question: Does God choose what is good because it is good, or is what is good good because God chooses it? (Plato's question talked about gods rather than God, and holy rather than good, but the basic point is the same.)

Consider the second possibility. If the good is simply what God chooses, then it seems the distinction between good and bad is arbitrary. What would stop God deciding that murder is good and kindness is wrong, for example? If good and bad are arbitrary in this way, then they lose their moral force.

Surely, then, the first option must be correct. God's choice of good and bad is not arbitrary. It is not the fact that he chooses the good that makes it good, he chooses the good because it is good. But that means that good things are good independently of God. God's choosing does not make them good – they are good already. That means their goodness does not depend upon God.

But if good and bad do not depend on God, that means we do not need God for there to be good and bad. If God doesn't exist, therefore, good and bad still can. So there is no dependency between God and goodness. So the existence of morality does not prove the existence of God and the non-existence of God would not threaten morality.

This argument is considered by many to be decisive. Some have tried to reply to it. For example, it is argued that God *is* goodness, so the question set out in the Euthypryo Dilemma is misleading. God doesn't choose what is good, God just is good. But then we could still pose the same basic dilemma in a different form: is God good because goodness is just whatever God is, or is God good because goodness is embodied in God? In other words, would God be good whatever its nature – all-loving or all-hating – or is God good because what it means to be good is fully manifest in God? The answers lead to the same conclusion: if goodness is not arbitrary, God's goodness must reflect the nature of goodness itself, which means that the concept of goodness is divorceable from that of God.

▶ Conclusion

The philosophy of religion is in some ways one of the most interesting areas in philosophy because it deals with big questions that trouble most of us at some time in our lives. But it is also a subject which is perhaps less interesting than it might be because of the continued interest in tired, often feeble, debates about arguments for God's existence, miracles and morality. If there are interesting philosophical questions about God then they are to be found around issues of the relationship between faith and reason, the conceptual coherence of the idea of God and what it really means to say that God exists. I have had to focus on some of what I consider to be the stale debates because this book is an introduction to the philosophy of religion as commonly taught. But perhaps it is time those setting the syllabuses found some more pressing questions to deal with.

Summary

The philosophy of religion explores the rational justifications for religious belief. In Western philosophy, these debates centre on the existence or non-existence of a God who is omnipotent, omnibenevolent and omniscient. One problem with this conception of God is that it seems it cannot be all these things given that there is evil in the world. Attempts to explain how the traditional conception of God can be reconciled with the existence of this evil are known as theodicies. The most well known theodicy is the free will defence, which says we need evil in order to truly exercise our free will.

Many believe that faith can step in to provide justifications for religious belief when reason cannot. James, for example, thought we were entitled to allow our passional natures to determine whether we believe in God, because God's existence cannot be proved or disproved yet it is a real possibility, its significance is enormous and we have to choose to believe or not. Pascal argued that we should believe in God because we cannot know if God exists, but it is a safer bet to suppose that it does.

Some people believe that religious language is different to normal language. It should not always be understood literally, but nor is it merely metaphorical or poetic. On a Wittgensteinian view, you only really understand religious language if you live within a community of believers and learn how to use it.

The ontological argument for the existence of God attempts to show that God must exist because the concept of a non-existent God is self-contradictory.

The main objection to this argument is that it jumps from truths about concepts to truths about real existence.

The cosmological argument attempts to show God must exist because the universe requires an uncaused first cause. Critics claim that we have no reason to suppose such a cause is necessary and even if it is, it is not clear why we should suppose this cause to be God.

The teleological argument states that God's existence is the best explanation for the high degree of order we see in the universe. Critics say that there is no evidence that this order is the product of rational design and that it can be explained though physics and evolutionary theory.

Some believe that religious experience is the main basis for religious belief. The problem with this as a justification for God's existence is that the fact that we feel something must be true is not usually considered a good reason for accepting that it is actually true. The public experience of miracles is not sufficient to justify belief in God because there is no good evidence to suppose such miracles have occurred.

It has been argued that God is required for morality to exist, but because the concepts of God and goodness can be separated, this claim seems to be untenable.

Glossary

Euthypryo Dilemma   Does God choose the good because it is good, or is the good good because God chooses it?

Faith   Belief which is not justified by reason.

Genuine option   The possibility to believe something which is a real possibility (a live option), that we must believe or not believe (a forced option) and is of great significance.

Immanent   With regard to God, existing within creation.

Miracle   Usually defined as something of religious significance which breaks the laws of nature, but sometimes as any event of religious significance.

Omnibenevolent   All-loving or all-good.

Omnipotent   All-powerful.

Omnipresent   Existing everywhere at all times.

Omniscient   All-knowing

Pascal's Wager   That given God's existence cannot be proved or disproved, it is a safer bet to believe in God than it is not to.

Problem of evil   The problem of reconciling the existence of God as traditionally conceived with the existence of evil and suffering.

Theodicy   An attempted solution to the problem of evil.

Transcendent   With regard to God, existing outside of creation.

Further reading

Aquinas's *Summa Theoligiae* and St Augustine's *Confessions* are two classic texts in the philosophy of religion, but the former, in particular, is not particularly approachable for the modern reader.

There are many introductions to the philosophy of religion. *The God of Philosophy* by Roy Jackson (TPM) and *The Puzzle of God* by Peter Vardy (Fount) are two of the best for a straight, syllabus-based approach. Coming from a different angle, *Arguing for Atheism* by Robin Le Poidevin (Routledge) is also an introduction but one with a rare, explicit non-believer's stance.

One of the most interesting modern writers on religion is Don Cupitt and his *The Sea of Faith* (SCM Press) is a brave attempt to construct a non-superstitious conception of religion which does not see God as having a real existence. Alvin Plantinga is also an interesting contemporary religious philosopher and *The Analytic Theist: An Alvin Plantinga Reader*, edited by James F. Sennett (Eerdmans William B. Publishing) is a good place to start.

5 Political Philosophy

▶ What is political philosophy?

Politics is a subject which divides people in many ways. It divides people according to their convictions, with people on the right, for example, often suspicious, disdainful or even loathing of people on the left, and vice-versa. It also divides people according to their interest, with some people seeing politics as by far and away the most important part of life, while others can't even see the point of walking down the road to vote once every five years.

These different reactions can perhaps be understood. Politics is about the way in which our society is ordered by its institutions, its rulers and its laws. In this sense politics surrounds us and determines how we can live on a day-to-day basis. People disagree in their convictions because people can have very different ideas about what the best way to live is. But people can also disagree about the importance of politics, because some see the political background to our lives as something we can ignore while we get on with living, whereas others are highly aware of the impact the political system has on many areas of our lives.

Political philosophy is about how we justify the various forms of government, political ideologies, laws and other features of the state. It is not the study of how different regimes and systems actually work, but an investigation into what principles and arguments can be used to support or criticise general forms of political institution and belief. Political philosophy thus delves beneath the hurly-burly of much political debate and examines more enduring questions.

Political philosophy is of interest not only to philosophers, but to students of politics and citizens interested in civic life. I would like to offer something in this chapter to all these potential readers. To do so will require us to look at a selection of topics which, though perhaps not typical of many undergraduate syllabuses, nevertheless touch on the major issues of rights, freedom and the legitimacy of the law. But to start with, we will look at some of the most important political ideologies.

▶ Liberalism

Liberalism may seem an odd place to start, especially for British readers, since in many Western countries the most powerful political parties describe themselves as socialist or conservative. In Britain, the Liberal Democrat Party and its successors have been in a distant third place for most of the last century.

But liberalism (with a small l) has been as successful in the West as the Liberal Democrat Party has been unsuccessful. The fact is that liberalism is the dominant political ideology of modern times and the socialist and conservative parties have accepted and worked within a broadly liberal framework. 'Liberal' may have become a term of abuse in some North American circles, but North America is still the liberal nation *par excellance*.

So what defines liberalism? Liberalism is based on the belief that individuals should have the freedom to live their lives as they see fit and that this freedom should be enjoyed by all members of society equally. In this way, the individual is of paramount importance. The interests of the state or the interests of a particular social class should never be used as a reason to restrict the freedom of individuals. In fact, the only justification for limiting the freedom of individuals is to safeguard the freedom of other individuals. As John Stuart Mill wrote in *On Liberty*: 'The only purpose for which power can be rightly exercised over any member of a civilised community, against his will, is to prevent harm to others.' People should not be forced to do things against their will for the common good. Nor should they be forced to do things for their own good if they don't want to. Nor should someone be forced to do something just because it is in the interests of a ruling class that they do it.

Understood in this way, we can see how Western democracy is essentially liberal in nature. The rights of the individual are often enshrined in constitutions and laws. Indeed, the idea of a liberal society is closely tied in people's minds to the idea of a democratic society. Countries where people are forced to work to further the state's interest or where slavery – official or unofficial – still exists are usually characterised as undemocratic or totalitarian. In fact, both these possibilities are compatible with democratically elected governments and a non-democratic government can institute a liberal regime. The trend, however, has been for more democratic societies to also be more liberal.

Liberalism is therefore a deeply entrenched feature of Western politics. But what is its justification? Several could be offered. One is that it is the ability to make autonomous, free choices for ourselves that is the most valuable characteristic humans have. It is what distinguishes us from other animals and gives our lives special value. Therefore, our political systems have to respect this faculty by allowing us to use it to the greatest degree possible. In this way, liberalism allows humans to flourish to their full potential, by maximising our capacity to enjoy freedom of choice.

A second cluster of arguments are based around the fallibility of human judgement and the plurality of human values. Arguments of this sort stress that no-one is able to say with any certainty that they know what the right way to live is. Further, it could be the case that human values are plural, which is to say that there is more than one way to live a good life. These two points, separately or combined, make a good case for saying that it is better to allow people, as far as is possible, to choose how to live their own lives than to impose a way of life on them. No-one else is in a position to decide what is best for other people, either because no-one has enough authority or because there is no one thing which is best for everyone anyway.

A third, more pragmatic, argument is just that society and individuals do much better if they live in a basically liberal society. It is no coincidence, it is argued, that liberal countries tend to be wealthier and more stable than their authoritarian counterparts.

Critics of liberalism often argue that it places too much stress on individual liberty. First, individuals may not be quite as free as we take them to be. Their so-called free choices are largely determined by their environments. For instance, the kind of free-market capitalism that tends to operate in liberal countries manipulates citizens to become voracious consumers, persuading them that they need to spend more and more to be happy. People are very much constrained by society and the liberal myth of the free, autonomous individual allows us to turn a blind eye to the many ways in which people are manipulated by corporate and government interests.

Second, individual liberty may well be a good, but liberals tend to overstate the importance of this good. We also need to be happy, to be able to live together in communities and to all enjoy a decent standard of living. Arguably, liberal societies sacrifice these goods for individual liberty. The stress on the individual erodes community life, weakening the bonds that tie society together. Inequality is tolerated as the price of freedom, which means millions live in poverty. Some would also argue that all this freedom is not making us happier. In fact, caught up in a consumerist free for all, we are often left unhappy because we cannot live up to the ideal of the perfect lifestyle sold to us by advertisers and the media.

These critiques of liberalism really call for a scaling down of the importance placed on individual liberty, not the end of liberalism altogether. Some critiques go even further. Religious fundamentalists sometimes argue that liberal societies are sinful, because they place more importance on individual liberty than God's law. In this way, liberal societies replace God with individual people, which is the height of human arrogance. Of course, one can only buy into this critique if one shares the fundamentalist convictions of those offering it, but it is worth at least being aware of this point of view, if only to understand the hostility Western liberalism faces in parts of the Islamic world in particular.

▶ Socialism

Although liberalism is the dominant political ideology of the West, others have also made their mark. Socialism is one of the most important. Like liberalism, socialism is really a broad family of political ideologies rather than a single one. It has been advocated by many democratic parties in the West and is also an important part of the communism of Marx, Lenin and Mao.

Socialism is best understood as a critical response to capitalism. In a capitalist society, individuals or corporations own and control the various forms of production, such as industry, transport and services. These corporations compete with each other to create the most profit for themselves. But the actual work that is needed in these industries is done by paid employees. So the people who do the work are not the people who own the capital – the assets and the profits of the companies.

What is more, in order to make more money, corporations have to become more and more cost effective. If one company is making a product which sells for five dollars, for example, a company in competition has to produce a better or a cheaper product. If it doesn't, it will lose out to the other company and eventually go bust. One of the easiest ways to cut costs and hence make more profit is to pay its workers less. Obviously, companies are not always cutting the wages of their employees. But it is the case that there is a constant pressure to keep wages as low as possible in order to maximise profit.

Socialism takes a look at this situation and declares it obviously unfair. Why should workers be paid as little as possible so that owners can earn as much as possible? Why should wealth be concentrated in the hands of the few owners and not spread in the hands of the masses who actually do the work? Surely, this is unjust?

The socialist answer is to ensure that the workers themselves control the means of production and that there is a fair distribution of profits among the whole workforce. If this happened on a company-by-company basis, there would still be a situation where some groups of workers would effectively have control over others, since the most successful companies would put a squeeze on the less successful ones. Perhaps for this reason, most socialists have argued that the state should take control of industry on behalf of all workers, thus ensuring a genuinely fair distribution of profits throughout the economy. A socialist society would thus ensure a fair society. As Marx put it, each would give according to their abilities and receive according to their needs.

It should also be noted that some associate radical socialism with dictatorships, largely because the Communist world was not (and is not where it still survives) democratic. But there is a long tradition of democratic socialism which utterly rejects this communist model.

The case for socialism is therefore largely a moral one. Socialism is fair, whereas its alternative is not. Does this mean we should all be socialists?

Arguments against socialism can be pragmatic or principled. Pragmatic arguments state that socialism may well be the ideal, but that in practice it just doesn't work. Any credible political philosophy has to start with the reality of human nature and the fact is that socialism runs counter to this. People do better whenever they strive as individuals for their own good. As a result, society does better when people are allowed to get on with it rather than have their affairs ordered by the state. This idea is put most forcibly by Adam Smith, who argued that when individuals each pursue their own interests, the interests of the whole are also served by what he called the 'invisible hand'. On this view, if we try and pursue the common good directly, we often fail. But if we pursue it indirectly, by each pursuing our own good, we find the goal is achieved.

Further, as Lord Acton said, power corrupts, and absolute power corrupts absolutely. Socialism requires a great deal of power to be placed in the hands of a few. Experience should have taught us that when this happens, people do not pursue the common good but look after themselves. Socialism thus faces a double disaster: those who have power have all the power and look after themselves. Meanwhile, the workers, who no longer see a link between the effort they put in and the wages they receive, lose the incentive to work hard.

These arguments are all pragmatic in that they are based on the idea that socialism, though a noble ideal, cannot succeed. There are also principled objections. These tend to be rooted in a vigorous defence of liberal individualism. It is of uttermost importance, it is argued, that people choose how to live their own lives. In a genuinely free society, if anyone wants to start a business and become a member of the owning classes, they can. If they would rather lead a quite life, work for an employer and draw a wage, they can. The socialist presents a caricature of society when she argues that people are divided up into owners (the bourgeoisie) and employees (the proletariat). In modern Western states, people can move between both classes, or even be a bit of both. For example, one can be an employee and yet own property. Further, many employees have more wealth than many owners. What's important is that people decide for themselves how to live rather than have their lives ordered by a too-powerful state that decides what is best for them.

▶ Conservatism

Intellectual debates about political theory have tended to focus mainly around liberalism and socialism. Yet one of the most powerful political forces is conservatism. Conservatism is essentially about preserving the institutions and social structures each generation inherits. It is not against change completely, but it argues against wholesale change, preferring instead a gradual evolution of social and political structures. Its enemy is therefore radicalism of any sort, attempts to bring about a root and branch reform of society in order to achieve a brighter tomorrow.

Conservatism has been justified in a variety of ways. For Edmund Burke (1729–1797), the basis of conservatism is that each generation is only a temporary custodian of society. Their duties lie not only to themselves, therefore, but also to other generations past and present. They should thus exercise caution before overturning their inheritance, which is the product of the cumulative wisdom of successive generations. There is something arrogant about any generation which thinks it alone has found the answers to society's ills and rejects all that has come before as outdated. They also have a duty to the next generations not to squander their inheritance, but to build upon it.

Apart from these arguments about responsibility, Burke also thought that continuity was essential for the smooth operation of society. If society changes too quickly, then by the time someone has been educated to be a good citizen, society has changed and they no longer know how to function in it. Hence, the preservation of existing structures, morals and institutions is a prerequisite for a harmonious society where everyone knows their place.

Conservatism can also be justified by a pessimistic view of human nature. Many conservatives think that human beings are essentially greedy, egotistic, self-serving and prone to error. Humans therefore need to be constrained by firm institutions and practices that keep their baser instincts in check. Traditional institutions are the best way of achieving this, since they provide order, certainty and continuity. It is foolish to think that we can do better by destroying the past and starting again because humans are neither wise nor benign enough to create moral and effective societies from scratch. Experiments in the Communist world provide evidence for this pessimistic credo.

The conservative philosophy is sometimes summed up in the principle that it is easier to destroy than to build. The present is the result of centuries of gradual evolution and we bring it down at our peril.

Critics of conservatism often point out that the institutions and practices that it aims to preserve often serve the interests of a narrow section of society. In Britain, for example, the second chamber of parliament still contains many people who are there simply because they inherited a title. Being born into the aristocracy gave these people an important role in the governance of the country. Conservatives who argue that we should not change the system are therefore supporting the interests of the aristocracy over those of wider society. Of course, the conservative will respond that the two are connected – preserving an institution like the House of Lords is not just for the benefit of the lords themselves, but for society as a whole. However, when in this, as in other cases, what is being directly preserved is the status of an elite, this defence can seem a little thin.

It can also be argued that conservatism can be used as a justification to preserve all sorts of terrible things. Slavery, for example, was defended on conservative grounds, as was the lack of votes for women. So it is evident that only the most hard-nosed of conservatives will refuse to admit society does need to change from time to time and sometimes such changes need to be quite radical. This means a credible conservatism might end up looking like little more than an urge to caution. Anything more may seem dangerously reactionary, resistant to any change in society, for good or for bad.

A final criticism is that conservatism fails to take account of the way in which the world as a whole is changing. Change for change's sake may be foolish, but the world is now so different to how it was even 20 years ago that to argue political institutions need not change very much could look like wishful thinking. Change is happening whether we like it or not and any political ideology which refuses to accommodate this is doomed to failure.

▶ Anarchism

Liberalism, socialism and conservatism are the three main political ideologies of recent history. A radical alternative, which has never been put into practice for more than short periods is anarchy – the absence of government.

Anarchists have an image of being violent rioters, punks or both. Anarchy is often used as a synonym for a lack of order or chaos. The image is unfortunate because the most eloquent of anarchist writers have demonstrated an optimistic idealism rather than a dark nihilism. Anarchism means the end of government, but for many anarchist thinkers, this would not mark a descent into chaos but a new dawn where people would live in harmony together, governed not by rules but self-restraint.

The anarchist position is based upon a rejection of the legitimacy of any kind of government. This can come from a perspective close to that of liberalism. Each person should be considered an independent, autonomous agent, capable of making their own choices. Anything which diminishes that autonomy needs to be justified. But whereas the liberal believes that some government is required in order to protect individual freedoms, the anarchist thesis is that any power the state takes on diminishes the freedom of individuals. Why is this so? According to Michael Bakunin, the reason is that government, by its nature, is the seizure of power by a minority to govern over the majority. Government is only government if it has power over those it governs. And if it has that power, it sets itself up as superior to the governed. Therefore, government by its very nature involves a dynamic of oppression.

Interestingly, anarchism had one of its periodic flourishes during the Russian Revolution. The anarchist Makhnovists disagreed with the communist Bolsheviks about the necessity to set up a form of central state socialism. It was always the dream of communism that the strong state would be a temporary measure and that after a while, once the new order had been established the state would just wither away. The Makhnovists argued that this was pure fantasy, and that power, once granted, tends to be retained. The Makhnovists lost out, but as history showed, they were at least partly right in that the Communist party maintained a strong grip on power in the USSR until its downfall in 1989.

The central plank of anarchist philosophy is therefore that one cannot cede power to any government without that power being misused. The only alternative is to work without government. This does not mean the collapse of society. On the contrary, society will be stronger because people will enter into entirely voluntary partnerships with each other. In the fashionable terminology of management consultants, social organisation will emerge from the bottom up, rather than being imposed from the top down. And, again in an echo of management consultancy, it is thought that such bottom-up arrangements will be more effective and durable.

A vital corollary of this is that anarchism would see private property abolished. The whole idea of private property only makes sense within a legal framework where property rights are guaranteed by the state. So if there is no state, there is no private property.

Anarchism can therefore be an extremely attractive prospect. But it faces difficulties, both practical and philosophical. Philosophically, the weakness of anarchism is that it is based on an extreme form of liberalism, where the freedom of the individual is more important than anything else. If we don't accept this basic premise, the intellectual case for anarchism weakens. If we accept, for example, that some things are more important than people not having their freedoms in anyway limited by state power, the strong anarchist objection to the state seems misguided. For instance, having to pay taxes may be a small price to pay for having good healthcare for all.

So it seems the case for anarchism must rest on its empirical claims about what actually is the most effective form of society. What we then need to judge is whether the anarchist is right in saying that the existence of the state will always lead to a situation where power is exercised by the few over the many and that this will be worse on balance than what would happen without the state. Most people think that this anarchist claim is highly implausible. Rather than co-operating happily together, most think that without the state, worse forms of oppression will arise. When the state goes, it is replaced with gangs and warlords. Lawlessness will not reduce oppression, it will merely allow new forms of oppression to thrive, without any external checks.

Anarchists reply that we only think this because we have been conditioned to think that the state is necessary. What we need to do is to relearn how to live without it. This claim is hard to test but even if we try to be as optimistic as possible, the anarchist vision does seem utopian.

However, some political theorists have taken a leaf from the anarchists' book. Libertarian philosophers such as Robert Nozick have agreed with the anarchists that any transfer of power from the individual to the state has to be justified and that the state has too much power at present. But they disagree that the state can be dispensed with altogether. More fundamentally, they see the right to retain the fruits of one's labour as central to human freedom and therefore at the very least property rights have to be protected by the state. Libertarians, therefore, argue not for an abolition of the state, but for a minimal state which does only what is strictly necessary to guarantee individual freedom. Libertarian arguments have been very important in academic political philosophy in the last quarter of the twentieth century and have also influenced the neo-liberal policies of conservative governments such as those of Ronald Reagan in the USA and Margaret Thatcher in the UK.

▶ Freedom

We have talked so far about freedom in several contexts. Freedom is rather like mother and apple pie. Everyone's for it and no-one is against it. But people disagree about just what freedom is. Socialists argue that their ideal society has more freedom than a capitalist one, whereas capitalists look on the large role of the state in socialist countries as an affront to freedom. How can everyone seem to both agree and disagree about the same thing at the same time?

The seeming paradox is largely a result of an ambiguity in the meaning or 'freedom'. Isaiah Berlin (1909–1997) distinguished between negative and positive freedom. Negative freedom is freedom from outside interference. It is the freedom to go about one's business without any external forces limiting what one does. It is called negative freedom because it is essentially an absence of coercion.

Positive freedom, on the other hand, is the freedom to do things, to live the best kind of life one can and to fulfil one's potential. It is called positive freedom because it is about what one can do as a result of having that kind of freedom. It is about being empowered to achieve something, or to be given the means to do so.

Although both forms of freedom merit the name, they are very different kinds of things and are often in conflict. For example, consider a pure capitalist society, without government support to the worst off in society. Such a society could have plenty of negative freedom. You could do what you want and no-one will stop you going about your business, as long as you don't interfere with the freedoms of others. If you want to live by the riverbank fishing all your life, you can (as long as someone else doesn't own it). If you want to try and run a big business and get rich, you can. Such a society could have very few external constraints and so could be negative freedom rich.

But what if you come from a poor family, or got ill and were unable to work as hard as other people? In such a situation, without any state to help you, you might find that you were unable to fulfil your potential. There would be many things you could, in other circumstances, do and achieve, but in a dog-eat-dog world, you just can't do them. Here, you are poor in positive freedom. There are no external constraints, but there is nothing to help you fulfil your potential and in the kind of society you're living in, without such help you are lost.

That's why in most Western societies we think the state should do more than just prevent people from interfering with each other. We should also help people to achieve their potential, by providing decent education, healthcare and housing, for instance. By doing this we can increase people's freedom to live the kind of life they choose without seriously diminishing their negative freedom. But there is some loss of negative freedom. At the very least, we need to tax income and profits to pay for the provision of these enabling services. This means interfering with the finances of individuals.

Isaiah Berlin cautioned, however, that positive freedom in particular was a concept that could be misused. In countries such as the old Soviet Union, governments interfered with people's negative freedom to an excessive degree in the name of positive freedom. Their claim was that in order for everyone to be free to fulfil their potential, strong state control of all areas of life was necessary. This was to misuse the word, for not only was it doubtful that the extreme form of government control exerted did significantly increase positive freedom, the price was too great a loss of negative freedom anyway.

Some libertarian philosophers would go further and say that it is a myth that positive and negative freedom have to be balanced. Rather, the best way to increase positive freedom is to increase negative freedom. In a society where the state intervenes very little, people are liberated to pursue their own interests in the knowledge that they will enjoy the full rewards. People who seem to need welfare and state benefits will actually find that their dependency is entirely learned and, freed from this unhealthy relationship with the state, they too will learn to stand on their own two feet with increased dignity. The very weakest in society will also be protected because humans are not nasty brutes and voluntary aid will ensure that no-one who needs help will lack it. In short, if the state steps back, people will be allowed to flourish and as a result, positive freedom will increase alongside negative freedom.

The libertarian position gained a lot of support in the wake of Nozick's powerful book, *Anarchy, State and Utopia* (1974). But many see the position as being unrealistic. Libertarians think life under the minimal state will be free and open, whereas critics think that life in such a world would be highly competitive, creating great differences between winners and losers. Those without capital, for example, will be unable to compete with the wealthy, who will inevitably own the majority of businesses and have access to the best education and healthcare, while the poor make do with the scraps that are made available by voluntary effort. In this way, libertarianism faces similar criticisms to those directed at anarchism. The ideal may sound fine, but critics doubt that things would actually turn out as the libertarian predicts.

Because the idea of freedom is so deeply entrenched in Western liberal politics, it is easy to forget that not everyone agrees that freedom is so important. In the United States, for example, the value of freedom is asserted as though it were the absolute good. When the USA goes to war, it is usual to hear that what is being defended is freedom.

But are we right to see freedom as of supreme importance? Many ethical theories place much value on other aspects of human life. Utilitarianism, for example, views the increasing of happiness and the diminishing of pain as being the main goals of ethics. If that is right, then we should not assume that maximising freedom is always the best way of achieving this. Certainly, many would agree that societies with a large degree of liberty for their citizens tend to flourish more than those where there is oppression. But this positive correlation may not hold under all circumstances. Increasing freedom may not always result in increases in other goods we value. It may even be the case that too much freedom has a bad effect. Implicit in the conservative philosophy, for instance, is the view that we need to have our behaviour checked by conventions and social rules to stop us descending into brutality. Many communitarian thinkers have also argued that we need the bonds, and with them the constraints, of community life in order to really flourish as individuals. Many of those who do not agree with the conservatives or the communitarians would none the less accept that it is too simplistic to say that freedom is the supreme good and it should be maximised at all cost.

▶ Justice

Another word which, like freedom, everyone lays claim to is justice. No-one ever rallied popular support by claiming they wanted to promote injustice. But as with freedom, justice means different things to different people and in different contexts.

Justice appears as a concept in different spheres of political debate. As its name suggests, distributive justice is concerned with how society ensures a just distribution of goods and benefits. These goods not only include wealth, but access to services and benefits as well as political and legal institutions.

Retributive justice, on the other hand, is concerned with punishment. It is sometimes called legal justice, since it is the kind of justice meted out by the law courts. We will look at this form of justice in the section on punishment (below). Here, we will look only at distributive justice, bearing in mind that this term covers a wide range of goods, not just money.

Since at least Plato, many have agreed that justice is something like everyone receiving their due. A society is just if everyone gets what they deserve, unjust if they do not. The problem with this definition, however, is that it is extremely 'thin'. That is to say, it tells us what the broad nature of justice is, but it leaves wide open exactly what 'receiving one's due' adds up to. For instance, does everyone get what they deserve if we allow people to go out and create as much wealth for themselves as possible, or for everyone to get their fair share do we need to redistribute wealth in some way, taking taxes from the rich to help the poor?

One person who thought justice required the second of these options was Karl Marx (1818–1883). Marx argued that the only just way to distribute wealth was to take 'from each according to his abilities' and to give 'to each according to his needs'. To see why he thought this, we need to first look at how wealth is distributed in a capitalist society. Here, the amount of money one receives bears no relation to the amount of work one needs to put in. Someone can go and work in an office for 40 hours a week and receive, say, 200 dollars. But their work could create a thousand dollars for the owner of the company, who works no harder, and perhaps works even less than the office worker. The rewards of labour can thus be vastly disproportionate. To Marx, this is obviously unfair, since in effect this means that one person (the owner) is allowed to keep the wealth generated by another (the worker).

An improvement on this system would be if each person were to be paid the fair value of their labour. On this model, society is like a huge co-operative. Each person pays into society a certain amount of their labour and is allowed to withdraw from it the equivalent cash value. But even this system is not entirely fair. Some people are born stronger or cleverer than others. These people may be able to work more or better, not because they make more effort, but just because they have more natural ability. These people would receive higher rewards than others, but only because of their unearned natural abilities. Further, some people need more than others. Someone with a disability, for instance, often requires some extra assistance just so that they can enjoy a normal amount of mobility. But if everyone is paid according to how much they work, these people will not receive the extra they need.

So we end up with Marx's principle that the only fair way to distribute wealth is to give everyone what they need and ask of everyone only what they can do. This is fair, because everyone does what they can, so no-one is having an easier time of it than anyone else. Also, everyone gets what they need, so no-one suffers just because their needs are greater.

Some of the problems with this view have already been dealt with in the section on socialism: the alleged impracticality of the socialist programme and the way in which it requires an unacceptable denial of individual liberty are the two main recurring themes here. In addition to these criticisms, others focus more directly on the ideal of justice in Marx, which is linked very closely to that of economic equality. Implicit in the argument is the idea that justice will involve an equal distribution of wealth, weighted slightly to take account of differing needs. But must justice be so solely tied to equality of economic outcome in this way? Isn't it at least plausible to argue that justice requires allowing people to keep the extra wealth they create for themselves if they choose to work for it? Shouldn't we allow people to benefit from their natural abilities, even if that creates inequality? At the very least, this might have practical benefits, since people are more likely to use their natural abilities to their greatest extent if they will be able to receive rewards for doing so.

The relationship between justice and economic equality is a major issue in political philosophy. Many have followed Marx in arguing the strong equality of outcome view: that justice requires everyone getting the equivalent quantity of benefits. Others stress equality of opportunity: that everyone should be given the same access to wealth and other social benefits, but how much they actually end up getting should be down to a combination of work, talent and maybe even luck.

One of the most important recent developments in this debate came with the publication of John Rawls's *A Theory of Justice* in 1971. Rawls's difference principle confronts one of the major difficulties with Marxist and socialist conceptions of justice. This problem is that, while equality of outcome does seem to be desirable, pursuing equality of outcome at all costs seems to be disastrous. For reasons already explained, it seems that we need to allow individuals the freedom to create wealth for themselves – and with it inequality – in order to fully harness the range of abilities in the workforce. Limiting personal reward seems to be a recipe for economic stagnation which harms the interests of everyone.

Rawls's difference principle attempts to accommodate what is true in both the socialist goal of equality of outcome and its critique. The difference principle states:

> All social values – liberty and opportunity, income and wealth, and the bases of self-respect – are to be distributed equally unless an unequal distribution of any, or all, of these values is to everyone's advantage.
>
> (John Rawls, *A Theory Of Justice*)

The principle is simple. Equality is to be preferred, but not if the price of equality is that everyone is worse off. It is better to have some inequality and have everyone better off than total equality where everyone is worse off. Crucially, we should only tolerate as much inequality as is strictly necessary to improve conditions for all. The difference principle is not a green light to allow any amount of inequality.

The major problem with Rawls's principle is that in order to apply it, one needs to know exactly what the effects of different policies will be on general well-being and equality. In theory, this should be an empirical matter – something which should be worked out by economists, perhaps. But in practice it is very difficult to say exactly what the effects on equality and well-being different polices have, especially since the principle does not just apply to crude wealth, but all social values. Hence, we find people adopting the difference principle to justify a wide range of wildly different political ideologies. Socialists, conservatives and libertarians can all claim that their approach results in the minimum amount of inequality required to improve the lot of everyone. Deciding who is right then becomes a very difficult matter.

▶ Rights

Along with freedom and justice, rights are something else which politicians of all stripes are keen to be seen to be defending. As with freedom, there are negative and positive rights. Negative rights are rights to non-interference. For example, the rights to free speech, freedom of association and free thought are all negative rights because in order to exercise them it is enough that no-one interfere with one's business. Positive rights, on the other hand, are rights to certain things, and for these rights to be maintained, it may be required that something be given or granted to someone. Rights to food, shelter and work are such positive rights.

Rights play an important part in contemporary political debate. Countries are sometimes refused recognition or access to trade if they do not guarantee basic human rights to their citizens. The United Nations Declaration of Human Rights is a document of paramount international importance, providing a benchmark against which regimes around the world are judged. There are also fierce debates about the number and scope of rights, with for example, 'pro-life' campaigners asserting the rights of the unborn child to life and the 'pro-choice' campaigners asserting the rights of the mother to choose what to do with her own body.

Rights are clearly important. But where do they come from? They are usually discussed as though they are somehow granted at birth to all human beings. On this conception, rights are 'natural'. We are born with them and to infringe them is to somehow breech a moral law of nature.

Many philosophers have found this conception of rights to be flawed. Rights just don't seem to be embedded in nature. Is a lion born with a right to hunt antelope? Does the antelope have any right not to be eaten by lions? These questions strike one as absurd, and considerations of this sort led Jeremy Bentham to declare that talk of natural rights is 'nonsense upon stilts'.

If rights aren't part of the fabric of nature, then they must therefore be a human construction. We are not born with rights. Rather, humans grant rights to other humans and sometimes also to other animals. Rights therefore need to be understood as legal rather than natural. They are legal in the sense that if they are not recognised by law, national or international, formal or common, they simply do not exist. We may well think something should be a right, but until it is legally recognised it is not a right. So, for instance, the right to join a trade union is a right which exists in some countries and doesn't exist in others. It is not a right that exists everywhere, but just is not recognised everywhere.

This conception of rights as non-natural fails to satisfy some because it is thought that if rights are a human construction, they do not have the strong force we usually attribute to them. For example, the right to life is considered absolutely fundamental. But if rights are granted by humans, then it seems we have the power to decide this isn't a fundamental right after all. This seems to conflict with the very nature of rights as basic and inviolable.

In response, it can be argued that it is just wrong to think that moral concepts, such as the concept of rights, have to be non-human in origin to have any force. The force rights have depends not on their origin, but on our determination to uphold or trample over them. Take the right to free speech as an example. Whether this right is respected or not ultimately depends on the decisions human beings make. These decisions have to be made whether the right is natural or non-natural. If rights were natural, that would give them no special protection.

However, what we think rights are based on might make a difference. Some would argue that rights are based on considerations of what is inviolable about persons. For instance, we may think that fundamental to our morality is the idea of the individual as a free, rational agent able to make decisions for herself and live her life as she wishes. We use the language of rights to make plain what this conception of a person entails. Because we value human life in this way, we say humans have a right to life, free thought, free movement, free speech and so on. In this way, rights embody what is non-negotiable and they would seem to have a strong, perhaps inviolable nature.

However, others, such as Bentham, think that rights are only granted because there are benefits in doing so. For example, a utilitarian such as Bentham would argue that the highest good is to increase happiness and decrease misery. As a means of achieving this, it may be useful to grant people certain rights. These rights offer basic guarantees, in law, which provide the secure and stable environment for people to go about their business in a way conducive to increasing the general happiness. However, it should be clear that on this conception of rights, it is always conceivable that the rights might be revoked. Rights serve a secondary role here, acting in the service of the primary goal of increasing happiness. If, therefore, circumstances arose where it would serve the general happiness if rights were removed, there would be no reason for the utilitarian to hold on to them. Rights on this conception do not represent anything funda-mental or inviolable. They are merely a mechanism used to achieve a higher goal.

Many would argue that this utilitarian conception does violence to the very concept of a right. Surely the whole point about a right is that it is something that cannot be taken away. But if rights are only justified by their usefulness, and this usefulness is not guaranteed to be permanent, rights become removable and, arguably, therefore not rights at all.

In defence of the utilitarian conception of rights, it is hard to see how many of the rights people now try and claim can be genuine if rights have to be inviolable in some way. For example, many would argue that in a rich, developed nation people have a right to decent housing. It is virtually impossible to make sense of this right if rights are inviolable. Surely one can only have a right to what is pos-sible and whether it is possible to have a decent home depends on when and where you are living, not on whether you are a human being or not. If a nation goes bankrupt, how can it maintain the right to provide decent housing for all? Yet if rights are inviolable and the right to decent housing is a genuine right, then it seems we have to accept that such a country would be breaching the rights of its citizens if it failed to uphold their right to decent housing.

There are two ways out of this dilemma. One is to say that many of these rights people claim are not genuine rights at all. Many, if not all, positive rights would, on this conception, be seen as bogus rights. The other way out is to say that rights are non-natural and violable. There is nothing wrong with saying that everyone has a right to decent housing, as long as we accept that this right is something granted by society on the basis of what it is currently possible for that society to do.

In conclusion, conceptions of rights can be weak or strong, broad or narrow. Weak conceptions of rights see them as secondary, serving a greater good and not of independent value in themselves. Such conceptions of rights allow in a broad range of rights. Strong conceptions see rights as inviolable, perhaps even natural. Such conceptions of rights tend to allow a narrower range of rights as genuine.

▶ The justification of the state and its authority

We have so far talked about different political ideologies and some of the key values which we expect to find in any political system. What we haven't yet considered is a more fundamental question: what justifies the state's existence, power and authority at all?

We are so accustomed to the existence of the state that it can be an odd experience to stand back and look at just what states do. They control vast areas of our lives, regulating them, taxing them, ordering them. States control our movements between countries, they run our education and health systems, they take around half of everything we earn in tax, they fight wars on our behalf. Yet many of us go from cradle to grave without seriously questioning their right to do these things.

There are questions about how much power a state should have, but to answer these it is best to start with the more fundamental question of what gives the state any authority at all. If we can decide on what basis the state should be granted authority, the extent of this authority should follow.

Thomas Hobbes (1588–1679) offered a simple reason for why the state should exist – without it life would be 'solitary, poor, nasty, brutal and short'. Hobbes took a dim view of human nature, seeing mankind as greedy, violent, competitive and vainglorious. We need a state to provide a stable structure to prevent a war of all against all.

On this view, the state is justified because of the benefits we gain from its existence. Bentham, though not sharing Hobbes's profound pessimism about human nature, agreed that the state is justified on the grounds of its usefulness. In his utilitarian view, we should always try and maximise happiness and diminish suffering. This goal can be achieved more efficiently if there is a state than if there is anarchy.

Hobbes and Bentham both offer an almost common-sense justification of the state: we may not like all it does, but we would much rather have it than be without it. But the answer sketched so far leaves many things unresolved. For instance, we may agree that we need a state, but how much authority and power need it have? Is the role of the state minimal – to stop us descending into violent anarchy, as Hobbes suggested – or does it have a wider role, acting in any area of life where its intervention produces a social benefit, as Bentham suggests?

A second question concerns the legitimacy of individual governments. It may be true that we need a state, but that does not provide any particular government with the legitimacy it needs to govern. For example, it is no good a harsh dictator saying that he has the right to rule because someone's got to do it. The point is that a different form of government would do the job better. Even if the dictator was doing the best job possible, we might still think that the dictatorship lacked legitimacy if it did not enjoy popular support. Despite what Bentham says, more seems required for a government to have legitimacy than the fact that the government's existence benefits us.

What we need, then, is not just an account of why states are necessary, but some kind of account of how any particular government is justified in exercising power over its citizens. One way of doing this is by means of the idea of the social contract.

Social contact theories appear in various forms in the history of political philosophy, but most famously in Rousseau's *The Social Contract* (1762). Contrary to Hobbes, Rousseau thought that life in the state of nature was something of a lost Eden, where people enjoyed complete freedom and lived together in harmony. The noble savage lived well. But humanity has become more developed and more complex, and there is now no turning back to a time of lost innocence. In order for people to flourish now, we have to trade in some of our freedom in return for the stability and security offered by the state. Where once each individual was sovereign over herself, now individuals pool sovereignty, handing it over the 'general will'. Our deal is that we cede personal sovereignty to the state on condition that everyone else does, to eliminate the need for conflict and to guarantee that we all are all on an equal footing.

The social contract is, of course, a fiction in that no-one literally signs over their sovereignty. The contract is tacit rather than explicit. But that is not to say the deal is not real. If the state abuses its power, it breaches the contract, and individuals have the right to fight against it. If an individual breaks their contract by acting outside of the law, the state has the right to withhold its privileges from her. The theory also has the advantage of allowing for varieties of political structure. Just as long as the contract is accepted by both sides, any form of government will do, from democracy to monarchy. This means the theory does not privilege a particular form of government preferred by Western nations.

The problem with social contract theories is that they are based on a metaphor that can break down. For example, what if I want to cancel my contract? I just don't seem to be able to do this. One cannot opt out of society. So if the state does have power by means of a contract, it seems to be a contract I have no choice but to sign. But a contract signed without free consent is not a contract at all.

Similar thoughts led Hume to reject contract theories. He thought that the idea that consent, implicit or explicit, lies behind the legitimacy of the state was absurd. Someone born in a country, only able to speak its language and without riches, for example, has no choice but to live there. The idea that a person consents to live under the rule of that nation by their tacitly agreeing to its terms is a myth. Like Hobbes, Hume thought the legitimacy of the state boiled down to the fact that we cannot live without it.

▶ Laws and law-breaking

The search for a fundamental justification for the state's existence perhaps has no better answer than this. It still leaves open the question of what form of government is best, be it democracy, monarchy, dictatorship or oligarchy. It also leave open the question of what kinds of laws the state should be allowed to enforce and what our obligations are to follow them.

The range of laws a state should be allowed to pass follows more or less directly from considerations of political ideology. Liberals usually follow Mill's principle that the state is only permitted to pass laws restricting the freedom of individuals to prevent harm to others. For socialists, the state needs to pass whatever laws necessary to ensure that the workers themselves control the means of production. For conservatives, laws should be passed which do not greatly extend nor diminish the role of the state nor radically change the nature of society (which is why Margaret Thatcher's Conservative government in Britain was not typically conservative at all.) Libertarians would want there to be as few laws as are necessary for society to function in an orderly way.

Whatever one thinks about the laws of a country and whether they are the best ones, there is always the question of how far one is justified in breaking them. In the Middle Ages, Aquinas, echoing a view which has been expressed throughout history, said that we have no duty to obey unjust laws. Indeed, he went so far as to say it is not permissible to obey a law if it contradicts God's law. Whether or not one believes in such a thing as God's law, most people would agree that it is more important to be moral than to follow the law. We admire people who refused to follow orders in Nazi Germany, even if it did mean breaking the law. And none of us likes to think that we would follow a law we believed to be deeply wrong. So it seems natural to believe that breaking laws – civil disobedience – is sometimes justified.

Yet at the same time, the whole point about the law is that it applies to everyone. If people simply followed their consciences and only obeyed the laws they agreed with, the law would cease to function as law. And without the rule of law – the law applying to everyone equally and fairly – society ceases to function. So if we accept the need for a state, and with it the need for laws, we have to accept that we may sometimes have to follow laws we disagree with.

Here, we have two contrasting views, neither of which seems quite right. It seems wrong to say that we should only follow laws we agree with, yet it also seems wrong to say we should always obey the law. To accommodate the reality of both these wrongs, we need to determine when it is permissible to break the law, given that we cannot say either that it is always or never right to do so.

John Rawls suggests there are three conditions which must hold for civil disobedience to be justified. The first is that the law being objected to is a substantial and clear injustice. We cannot permit people to break the law to protest against any law they think is wrong. In order to maintain the rule of law, civil disobedience needs to be reserved for protests against serious injustices only. Second, civil disobedience should only take place when legal avenues have been exhausted or where it is evident that there are no legal means of remedying the unjust law. This stress on following legal routes whenever possible again ensures that the general rule of law is upheld. Rawls's third condition is roughly that the act of disobedience must not undermine society so as to cause more harm than obeying the unjust law would. The idea here is that civil disobedience is only justified if the result is a fairer and more just society. So one needs to be careful that the net result of any protest will achieve this.

Rawls, following Martin Luther King, argued that civil disobedience must be a public act. Secretly not paying your taxes does not count, because that does not have the goal of ending an injustice – it simply has the aim of you personally avoiding an alleged injustice. Further, by making the protest public and facing up to the legal consequences of breaking the existing law, you uphold the general principle of the rule of law. This is essential if the protest is to be seen as a genuine attempt at reform, rather than an overthrow of the whole system. Protests should also be proportionate. For example, it would be wrong to use violence as part of one's protest if one's aims could be achieved by peaceful means.

Rawls's principles would satisfy many who are more or less happy with the system they live in and wish to reform it from within. But those who see the societies they live in as being more radically corrupt may find his arguments weak. Anyone convinced, for example, that a class war is necessary to overturn the capitalist exploitation of the workers is unlikely to think that peaceful protest over individual unjust laws is a sufficient form of protest. If the whole system is corrupt, then the whole system needs overturning. Rawls's principles only seem to apply to situations where the system as a whole is basically acceptable.

▶ Justifications for punishment

The state does not just pass laws, it also punishes those who break them. But what are the justifications for punishment? There are essentially four: retribution, deterrence, protection and rehabilitation.

Retribution is basically revenge. Punishment is justified on these grounds because injured parties have the right to 'get their own back' on those who harmed them. There are many reasons why we might want to strike back when people wrong us, including the desire to stop that person doing wrong again or to send a signal to others that such behaviour will not be tolerated. But retribution is not justified on these other grounds. It is justified purely on the grounds that we have a right to harm those who harm us.

On the one hand, retribution seems vital to common-sense notions of justice. It just strikes us as wrong that someone can cause harm and not have to face up to any kind of punishment for it. But it can equally seem cold and barbaric to insist on retribution if no good is achieved by it. What is the point of punishing someone purely for the sake of revenge if it doesn't stop other harms occurring?

For this reason, many are unpersuaded that retribution is a sufficient reason for punishment.

Deterrence is often given as another justification. We need to punish wrong-doers in order to deter other people from doing similar wrongs. If people are put in prison for robbing banks, that will make anyone else thinking about robbing a bank think twice. But if people were not punished for robbing banks, we would surely see banks being robbed all the time.

The deterrence argument faces some difficulties. First, it is not clear how much sentences affect the deterrent. For example, many people argue that we need the death penalty (capital punishment) for murderers on grounds of deterrence. But the evidence seems to suggest that what deters criminals is the thought that they will get caught rather than the exact nature of the sentence they would face. So although we need punishment in general as a deterrent, the nature of that punishment still needs to be decided.

A more serious problem is that the deterrence argument justifies punishment on the grounds of the crimes it will stop. But, of course, the punishment is given to the person who has already committed a crime. So the criminal is being punished, not for what they have done, but in order to stop other people doing the same. This seems unsatisfactory, because surely punishment needs to be for the wrongdoing itself, not some other purpose.

One way around this could be to combine the deterrence and retribution arguments. Retribution seems to be an exercise in justice, but if it leads to no good consequences, it seems futile. The deterrence aspect provides that missing benefit. On this view, punishment is retribution rightly taken because it will produce a benefit, which is the deterrence of future crimes.

A third justification for punishment is to protect the public. If someone is a killer, they need to be kept locked up in order to protect others. This justification follows the classic liberal position that someone's liberty may be curtailed in order to prevent harm to others. Although there seems to be little to object to here, it does need to be born in mind that many instances of punishment could not be justified in this way. Most murders, for instance, are not committed by people eager to kill again, but are one-off acts by people driven to desperate hatred against a particular individual. There is also the problem that prison tends to make people more criminally minded than when they were first put away. Prisons are almost crime schools. So if we want to protect ourselves, it seems making a lot of people who have done something wrong live in close proximity to other wrongdoers, so they can become even more imbued in the criminal life, is a pretty poor way of doing so. Protection is thus a perfectly good justification for punishment, but not necessarily of the extent and manner of actual punishment today.

A final justification of punishment is for the rehabilitation of the criminal. We can't undo what the criminal has done, but we can reform the criminal and ensure that they go on to become decent members of the community. This view also faces difficulties. First, as with the protection argument, not all criminals need to be reformed. Many committed their crimes under special circumstances and are no more likely to repeat their offence than anyone else. Also, if the aim of punishment is to reform, then aren't we more justified in punishing people who haven't yet offended, but have all the characteristics of a potential offender, than we are in punishing someone who did wrong in a moment of weakness? This seems unacceptable because we think we should only punish those who have actually done wrong. But if reform is the justification of punishment, why should it be limited in this way?

As with deterrence, we could perhaps get around this by combining the justification with the retribution argument. Punishment could be justified as retribution properly taken because of the positive end result of reform of the criminal.

It is likely that any credible theory of punishment would draw on arguments for retribution, deterrence, protection and rehabilitation. It is not to be expected that one argument alone could justify all forms of punishment. It also seems likely that any proper defence of punishment will lead to conclusions that conflict with our current penal practices. It is one thing to justify punishment, quite another to justify current policy on punishment.

▶ Conclusion

The main questions of political philosophy overlap and inform each other in many ways. In order to maintain a consistent position it seems necessary to fix upon some basic principles. This is why issues of political ideology are so important and so divisive. If one is a liberal, for example, this will affect quite directly the ways in which one sees the proper scope and power of the state, the role of punishment and the proper use of concepts like freedom, rights and equality. A socialist's view of all these issues will also be informed by their basic socialist commitments, but they will be led to often very different answers.

At the same time, faith in the power of ideology is at an all-time low. Most people now seem to think we need to be less ideological. In Western politics we hear a lot about pragmatism, about doing 'what works', unhindered by ideological constraints. Political philosophy can perhaps serve as a caution that this kind of thinking can only go so far. We cannot untie questions of basic ideology from questions of economic justice, freedom and state authority. If we seem to be able to do this, it can only be because our fundamental ideology (a form of liberalism) is so embedded in our culture that we hardly notice it is there.

It is very important we do not forget it is there. We need to constantly subject our ideological commitments to rational scrutiny to make sure we do not fall into error. What is more, we cannot begin to understand the conflicts in worldviews between fundamentalist religions of all kinds and Western liberal democracy unless we recognise the fact that the ideology we accept is not accepted by all. To do that effectively we need to see clearly what our ideology is and how it differs from those of its critics. Political philosophy can help in this because it analyses and lays bare the ideas, arguments and concepts that form these ideologies. For that alone, the subject is well worth our attention.

Summary

Political philosophy is concerned with issues such as how we justify the existence of a state, what form and powers a state should have and what principles governments should follow.

The dominant political ideology in the West is liberalism, which stresses the rights of individuals to choose for themselves how to live their lives. Liberalism is based in the idea that our freedom to choose is an important part of what gives human life value, that there are many values one can live by, and that no-one has the knowledge or right to choose how everyone else should live. Critics claim liberals place too high an importance on human freedom as compared to happiness, welfare and solidarity.

Socialism is a reaction against the tendency of capitalist societies to concentrate wealth in the hands of the owners and away from the workers who actually produce the wealth. Socialists claim a fairer society is one where the workers own the means of production and enjoy a fair share of the wealth created. Critics claim that socialism is idealistic because people will always prefer to look after themselves more than society as a whole. They also say that socialism requires taking away too much liberty from individuals.

Conservatives are against radical change and believe it is important to preserve and maintain existing structures of society in order to safeguard our inheritance and allow for society to develop in a gradual and manageable way. Critics claim conservatism preserves the privileges of elites, can preserve unjust practices, and fails to accommodate the fact that the world is now changing faster than ever.

Anarchists are opposed to any form of government and private property on the basis that no-one has the right to have power over others. Anarchists have an optimistic view of human nature and believe that without government, co-operation will ensure a stable and happy society. Critics claim anarchism is utopian, although libertarians agree with it to a certain extent, in that they believe the role of the state should be absolutely minimal.

An important concept in politics is freedom. Freedom can be positive – the freedom to do something or to fulfil one's potential – or negative – freedom from outside interference. Both forms of freedom are desirable, but they may sometimes be in conflict with each other.

Distributive justice is everyone getting their fair share of society's goods. Many believe that a fair share is an equal share, of either actual outcomes or opportunities to obtain these outcomes. Rawls has argued that inequality is just only if the existence of that inequality makes everyone better off than they would be if things were more equal.

Rights can be negative (rights of non-interference) or positive (rights of access to services or goods). Some believe rights are natural, others that they are non-natural but inviolable, and others that they are only used by us as a means to achieve other goods and have no real existence or value independently of these purposes.

The existence of the state has been justified in several ways. One is that we need the state to prevent society from descending into chaos. Another is that the state is legitimised by an implicit contract between the citizen and the state whereby citizens hand over their individual sovereignty to the state in return for its protection.

The right to break the law if a law is unjust is upheld by most. However, for such civil disobedience to be justified, it must meet several conditions. Rawls has argued that these are that the law being objected to is a clear and major injustice, that all legal avenues have been exhausted and that the overall effect of the protest is a more just society.

States punish law-breakers to deter other people from breaking the law, to punish law breakers themselves, to reform criminals or to protect the public. The extent to which any of these provide a satisfactory justification for punishment is much contested.

Glossary

Authority A state or government has the authority to act on behalf of its citizens when it has a legitimate justification to exercise that power.

Autonomy The capacity an individual has to make free choices for themselves.

Capital Wealth, either in money or assets.

Capitalism The system whereby capital is owned by whichever private individuals are most efficient at generating and keeping it.

Civil disobedience Breaking the law in order to protest about a law which one feels to be unjust.

Communism A form of socialism where the state has ownership of the means and output of production.

Legitimacy   An action is legitimate if it is exercised in accordance with legal or moral law.

Libertarianism   The view that the role of the state should be minimal to allow as much freedom to individuals as possible.

Power   Power is an ability to force one's will on others, whether or not one has the legitimate authority to do so.

Further reading

Some classic and accessible texts in political philosophy include Plato's *Republic*, John Locke's *Two Treatises of Government*, Rousseau's *The Social Contract*, Mill's *On Liberty* and Marx and Engel's *The Communist Manifesto*.

Perhaps the two most important contemporary works of political philosophy are John Rawls's *A Theory of Justice* (Oxford University Press), which is now a classic liberal text, and Robert Nozick's *Anarchy, State and Utopia* (Blackwell), which heralded an era of great popularity for libertarianism. Roger Scruton's *The Meaning of Conservatism* (Palgrave) is pretty self-explanatory while G. A. Cohen continues to write passionately on socialism. His *If You're an Egalitarian, How Come You're So Rich?* (Harvard University Press) is good value just for the title.

Political Thought, edited by Michael Rosen and Jonathan Wolff (Oxford University Press) is a superb reader and if you were only to buy one more book on political philosophy, this should probably be it. If it's going to be two, add Wolff's *An Introduction to Political Philosophy* (Oxford University Press).

Glossary

A glossary for each text is found at the end of each chapter. Here are a few more general philosophical terms that are found throughout the text.

Abduction   Argument to the best explanation.

A posteriori   Reasoned from experience.

A priori   Reasoned from first principles, the truth of which are not established by the evidence of experience.

Contingent   Not necessarily the case or true.

Deduction   A form of reasoning where, if the premises are true, the conclusion must also be true.

Empiricism   The style or school of philosophy which takes as the starting point of knowledge the data of experience.

Epistemology   The branch of philosophy concerned with questions of knowledge and its foundations.

Existentialism   The style or school of philosophy which takes as its starting point the idea of the necessity for humans to choose their own values.

Induction   A form of reasoning that uses the experiences of the past or future as evidence for truths about the past, present or future that cannot be established by more direct means.

Logical positivism   An early twentieth-century approach to philosophy which claimed that anything which could not be verified by logic or by experience was meaningless.

Premises   The starting points of arguments, from which conclusions are derived.

Rationalism   The style or school of philosophy which believes the most important and fundamental truths can be established by the correct operation of reason, without reference to experience.

Realism   The view that things have an existence independent of human thought and consciousness. One can be a realist about a number of things, including the external world, morality and beauty.

Sound   An argument which is both valid and the premises of which are true.

Valid   A successful deductive argument where the truth of the conclusion follows necessarily from the truth of the premises.

Further Reading

Suggestions for further reading for each theme are provided at the end of each chapter. Here are a few more general recommendations.

The companion volume to this book is *Philosophy: Key Texts* (Palgrave Macmillan). It adopts a similar approach to this book but looks at works by Aristotle, Descartes, Hume, Russell and Sartre.

The Philosophers' Magazine, which I edit, is a quarterly aimed at general readers as well as professionals. Its website is www.philosophers.co.uk

The best single-volume reference book on the subject is the *Oxford Companion to Philosophy*, edited by Ted Honderich (Oxford University Press).

If you want to start reading original philosophical texts, the best place to start is probably with Nigel Warburton's excellent anthology, *Philosophy: Basic Readings* (Routledge).

The Philosopher's Toolkit, by Julian Baggini and Peter S. Fosl (Blackwell) is a comprehensive guide to the techniques of philosophical thinking and argument.